Tested by Time

A Collection of Charleston Recipes

Published by Porter-Gaud Parents Guild
Copyright Porter-Gaud Parents Guild
P.O. Box 30431
Charleston, South Carolina 29417

Designed, edited, and manufactured by
Favorite Recipes® Press
an imprint of

FRP

P.O. Box 305142
Nashville, Tennessee 37230
1 (800) 358-0560

Book Design: Brad Whitfield and Susan Breining
Art Director: Steve Newman
Project Editor: Ashlee G. Brown
Gate Illustration: James L. Mojonnier

Library of Congress Number: 97-92372
ISBN: 0-9658842-0-1

Manufactured in the United States of America
First Printing: 1997   15,000 copies

To order additional copies of this book contact:
Tested by Time
Porter-Gaud Parents Guild
Cookbook Sales
P.O. Box 30431
Charleston, South Carolina 29417
Toll Free: (800) 274-8191
Phone: (803) 723-0015
Fax: (803) 769-7668

PREFACE

Since 1670, one of Charleston's most valued and well-known traditions has been its extraordinary devotion to culinary excellence. Rich in fresh fruits, vegetables, and seafood, Charleston owes much of its character and cuisine to those who settled here in the first 200 years. Loyal subjects of Charles II, of course, established the initial Carolina colony, Charles Town, and later Louis XIV denied Protestants religious freedom, driving the Huguenots out of France to the Lowcountry. Africans have likewise had a profound impact on the Lowcountry and its cuisine. Our early Charleston kitchens took keen advantage of these French Huguenot, English, and African cooks and their special knowledge of how best to employ the local harvest—especially "Carolina Gold," as Europeans referred to our Lowcountry's superlative rice crop.

Drawing on this heritage, then, our editors have joined old and new recipes for shrimp, oysters, crab, and fish—all found in abundance in this seaport—with delicate, garden-fresh vegetables and herbs, lean cuts of meat, and today's healthiest cooking techniques. Grilling poultry and seafood, dining alfresco, and capturing the ambience of Charleston at mealtime are all parts of this "cookbook"—as are the most sensational dessert recipes we've ever seen (fat-free or not, they are mandatory).

Recipes for dishes long indigenous to Charleston are here, but so are dozens of others long enjoyed by Charleston families of varied heritages. Indeed, new residents drawn to Charleston's climate and beauty over the last several decades have added an inspiring breadth and variety to Charleston's table. And these, too, have found a place in this collection.

Every "receipt" has thus been tested by time and by dedicated Porter-Gaud volunteers. We wish you and yours much enjoyment.

Cookbook Advisory Committee

Anne O. Long
*Parents Guild President
1997-99*

Kay Maybank
*Parents Guild President
1995-97*

Janice Waring
*Parents Guild President
1993-95*

Mary Ann Asbill
Cookbook Co-Chair

Karen Elsey
Cookbook Co-Chair

Vicky Horres
Advisor

Jackie Valicenti
Advisor

Recipe Collection
Suzanne Jernigan
Jackie Valicenti
Beth Renken
DarLyn Harris

Marketing
Sandra Bruenner

Special Events Coordinator
Croft Lane

Proofreading
Nina Hershon

Newsletter
Kate Johnson
Emily Kenan-Hegamyer

Testing/Tasting
Edith Blair
Sally West

Editing
Liz Thompson

Treasurer
Mary Ann Knight

Special Thanks

South Carolina Historical Society

The Charleston Museum
for their exquisite historical postcard collection

The Local Chefs and Restaurants
for sharing some of their favorite recipes

Porter-Gaud Families and Friends
for their enthusiastic support

Robert Stockton
*for his insightful
commentaries*

Leonard L. Long, Jr.
for his creative direction

Karen Bacot
for her graphic expertise

INTRODUCTION

Tested by Time seemed like such a fitting title for the Porter-Gaud School Parents Guild cookbook. Charleston has, of course, withstood the test of time—as well as hurricanes and earthquakes. Indeed, for more than 300 years, this city's charm has survived the ages essentially intact. And while Charleston is, architecturally, a living museum, its distinctive, ever-evolving cuisine remains equally irresistible.

Porter-Gaud has long played a role in Charleston's vibrant history. Our preparatory school lies along the banks of the Ashley River overlooking Charleston's harbor. It represents more than a century of experience in nurturing young minds, helping teach not just history and literature, but honor and how to live a life. Formed in 1964 by the merger of the old Porter Military Academy with two of Charleston's most distinguished schools, the roots of Porter-Gaud date to 1867.

These "receipts" from Charleston should likewise stand the test of time. Many have been passed along to us (and now you) with loving care, with remembrances of good times. Others are of far more recent vintage, and emphasize today's focus on fresh local ingredients.

Special thanks must go to the cookbook committee chairs and committee workers without whose endless hours of dedication this project would have never risen beyond a concept.

Anne O. Long, *President*
Porter-Gaud Parents Guild

TABLE OF CONTENTS

DOCK STREET THEATRE

Charleston's theatre tradition goes back to 1705, when Tony Astin, an English poet, playwright, and actor, presented the first known production. The original Dock Street Theatre, which was the first building in America erected for theatrical performances, was built on Dock (now Queen) Street, near Church Street, about 1735. The theatre burned a few years later.

Subsequently, the site was occupied by the Planter's Hotel, one of the city's top hostelries of the antebellum period. Tradition says that Planter's Punch originated there. By the early twentieth century, the hotel was in ruinous condition. Preservationists prevented its demolition, however, and in 1935 it was rehabilitated by the City of Charleston as a Works Progress Administration project.

The present Dock Street Theatre, a reconstruction of an eighteenth-century theatre, was built in the courtyard of the former hotel, and the old hotel lobby serves as the entrance to the theatre. The Dock Street Theatre at 135 Church Street is used for a variety of cultural events, including Spoleto performances.

Cocktail Fare

Dock Street Theatre. Opened in 1736. Charleston, S. C.

COCKTAIL FARE

CROUSTADES

**Thick homemade-quality
white bread
Melted butter**

Cut bread slices with a
biscuit cutter into circles
slightly larger than the cups
in miniature muffin tins.
Spread the melted butter
over 1 side of the circle with
a pastry brush. Press buttered-
side down into the miniature
muffin cups, shaping into
a cup. Bake at 350 degrees
for 10 minutes or until
light brown.

ARTICHOKE CROUSTADES
Serves Twenty-Four

1 (14-ounce) can artichoke hearts,
  drained
1 cup mayonnaise

²/₃ cup grated Parmesan cheese
Salt, pepper and thyme to taste
Croustades (at left)

Chop the artichokes coarsely by hand or in a food processor. Add the mayonnaise, cheese, salt, pepper and thyme, tossing gently to mix. Pipe or spoon the mixture into the Croustades. Place on a baking sheet. Bake at 350 degrees for 5 to 10 minutes or until hot and bubbly. Serve immediately.

· · · · ·

SMOKED GOUDA AND
CARAMELIZED ONION QUESADILLAS
Serves Twenty-Four

2 medium onions, thinly sliced
1 tablespoon brown sugar
¹/₄ teaspoon white wine vinegar
2 tablespoons butter
1¹/₂ cups grated smoked Gouda
  cheese

3 ounces sliced prosciutto, chopped
4 (10-inch) flour tortillas
Freshly grated black pepper
2 tablespoons melted butter

Sauté the onions with the brown sugar and vinegar in 2 tablespoons butter in a skillet for 20 minutes or until golden brown, stirring frequently. Cool. Layer the cheese, prosciutto and onions over half of each tortilla. Sprinkle with pepper. Fold each tortilla in half to enclose the filling; brush with the melted butter. Brush a large skillet with melted butter. Cook the quesadillas in the skillet over medium-high heat for 2 minutes on each side or until brown spots appear. Remove to a baking sheet. Bake at 350 degrees for 5 minutes or until golden brown and the cheese is melted. Cut each quesadilla into 6 triangles. Serve hot.

BLACK OLIVE PASTE

5 to 6 large sprigs fresh
   rosemary
4 to 5 large sprigs fresh
   thyme
1 cup black calamata or
   Greek olives, pitted
1 cup canned, low-salt black
   olives, pitted
3 cloves of garlic, minced
$^1/_3$ cup olive oil
Pepper to taste

Cut off the rosemary leaves
and pull off the thyme leaves,
discarding stems. Combine
the olives, rosemary, thyme,
garlic, olive oil and pepper
in a food processor container.
Process until coarsely
chopped. May store in the
refrigerator for 4 to 6 days.
May freeze with a small
amount of olive oil added to
the top. Since calamata olives
are very salty, adding low-salt
black olives reduces the salty
flavor. Use as a topping for
bruschetta, pizza, bread or
crackers, or use in pasta
salads, vegetarian burritos or
pocket sandwiches.

BLACK AND GREEN PIZZA
Serves Twelve

12 spears fresh asparagus
1 large unbaked pizza crust
$^3/_4$ cup Black Olive Paste (at left)
12 thin strips red bell pepper

12 thin strips yellow (or green) bell
   pepper
$^1/_2$ to $^3/_4$ cup shredded fresh
   Parmesan cheese

Trim the asparagus. Cook in a steamer until tender-crisp. Place the pizza crust on
a pizza pan lightly sprayed with nonstick cooking spray. Spread the Black Olive
Paste over the crust, leaving $^1/_2$-inch rim. Arrange the asparagus on the crust,
spacing evenly and pointing the tips toward the center. Arrange the bell pepper
strips between the asparagus spears, gently bending so they lie flat. Sprinkle with
the cheese, including the rim of the crust. Bake at 400 degrees for 8 to 10 minutes
or until the cheese is melted and the crust is light brown. Let stand for 5 minutes.
Cut into wedges with the asparagus in the center of each slice. Serve hot or cold.

• • • • •

SPOLETO CANAPÉS
Makes Sixty-Four

$1^1/_2$ cups shredded sharp Cheddar
   cheese
1 cup mayonnaise
1 cup chopped green onions
1 teaspoon curry powder

1 teaspoon pepper
$1^1/_2$ cups chopped black olives
8 English muffins, split, cut
   into quarters

Combine the cheese, mayonnaise, onions, curry powder, pepper and olives in a
bowl and mix well. Spread on the English muffin quarters. Place on a baking
pan. Bake at 350 degrees for 10 minutes or until the cheese is melted.

TORTILLA ROLL-UPS
Makes Forty

8 ounces cream cheese, softened
1 cup sour cream
1/2 envelope taco seasoning mix
1/8 teaspoon garlic powder
1/4 teaspoon chili powder, or
   to taste
1 (4-ounce) can chopped green
   chiles

1 (4-ounce) can chopped black
   olives
1 cup finely shredded sharp
   Cheddar cheese
1/2 cup chopped green onions
   (optional)
5 (10-inch) flour tortillas

Combine the cream cheese, sour cream, taco seasoning mix, garlic powder and chili powder in a bowl and mix well. Add the green chiles, olives, Cheddar cheese and onions and mix well. Spread a thin layer of the mixture over each tortilla. Roll to enclose the mixture. Wrap each roll in plastic wrap. Store in the refrigerator for at least 1hour. Cut into 1-inch slices, discarding the end pieces. Place on a lettuce-lined serving plate. May substitute low-fat cream cheese for the cream cheese and low-fat sour cream for the sour cream.

· · · · ·

ROSIE'S FOCACCIA
Serves Eight

1 large eggplant, cut into 1/4-inch
   slices
Salt to taste
1 onion, thinly sliced
4 cloves of garlic, crushed
1/4 cup plus 2 tablespoons olive oil
1 recipe pizza pastry

6 to 8 ripe plum tomatoes, thinly
   sliced
1/4 teaspoon freshly ground pepper
2 to 3 tablespoons chopped fresh
   oregano
1 cup shredded mozzarella cheese

Sprinkle the eggplant slices lightly with 1 tablespoon salt. Let stand on paper towels for 20 minutes to drain. Pat with paper towels to dry. Sauté the eggplant with the onion and garlic in 1/4 cup olive oil in a skillet until limp but not brown. Spread the pizza pastry onto a pizza pan. Brush with the remaining 2 tablespoons olive oil. Layer the tomato slices and sautéed vegetables over the dough. Sprinkle with pepper, oregano and cheese. Bake at 450 degrees for 15 to 20 minutes or until golden brown. Cut into small wedges. May substitute 1 tablespoon dried oregano for the fresh oregano.

ROASTED EGGPLANT AND PEPPER APPETIZER
Serves Six

1 medium eggplant
Salt
Olive oil
2 tablespoons dried basil
1 red Holland pepper
1 yellow Holland pepper

1 green bell pepper
Fresh or bottled pesto
1 French bread baguette
2 to 3 plum tomatoes, sliced
8 ounces mozzarella cheese, thinly
   sliced

Cut the eggplant into 1/4-inch slices. Layer in a colander with a sprinkle of salt on each layer. Let stand for 30 minutes. Pat dry with paper towels and brush off excess salt. Brush a large baking sheet with olive oil; sprinkle with basil. Place the eggplant slices on the baking sheet, turning to coat each side with basil and olive oil. Bake at 350 degrees for 30 minutes or until tender and light brown. Place the whole peppers on a broiling rack. Broil for 15 to 20 minutes or until blistered and dark, turning frequently. Place the peppers in a paper bag and seal. Let stand for 30 minutes. Peel and seed the peppers under cold running water. Pat dry with paper towels. Cut into 3/4-inch strips. Cut the baguette into two 6 to 8-inch pieces; split lengthwise. Spread the pesto over the cut side of the baguette. Layer the eggplant, peppers, tomatoes and cheese on the bottom halves. Arrange all the baguette halves cut side up on a baking sheet. Bake at 400 degrees for 3 minutes or until the cheese is melted. Place the top halves on the bottom halves. Cut into servings. Serve hot. Eggplant and peppers may be prepared ahead and refrigerated. Store the roasted peppers in a jar of olive oil.

• • • • •

CAESAR MUSHROOMS
Serves Four

2 anchovy fillets, chopped
1/2 teaspoon salt
1/2 teaspoon freshly ground black
  pepper
1/2 cup olive oil

1/4 cup lemon juice
4 cloves of garlic, chopped
8 ounces portobello mushrooms,
   thickly sliced

Mash the anchovy fillets with the salt and pepper in a bowl. Add the olive oil, lemon juice and garlic and mix well. Place the mushrooms in a shallow dish. Pour the anchovy mixture over the mushrooms. Marinate, covered, in the refrigerator for several hours; drain, reserving the marinade. Cook the mushrooms on a hot grill for 3 to 4 minutes on each side. Serve with cocktail picks. May mix the mushrooms with romaine lettuce and use the reserved marinade as a salad dressing or serve the mushrooms as a side dish with grilled meat.

SHERRY SLUSH
Serves Eight

3 cups water
1 cup sugar
3 cups orange juice
1 cup grape juice
1 1/2 cups sherry, or to taste

Combine the water and sugar in a saucepan. Boil over medium heat for 10 to 15 minutes or until the sugar syrup thickens, stirring frequently. Add the orange juice, grape juice and sherry. Pour into a freezer container. Freeze, covered, for 24 hours or longer. Let stand in the refrigerator for 2 to 3 hours to become slushy before serving. Serve in pretty glasses garnished with mint.

Portobello Mushroom Sandwiches
Serves Variable Amount

Portobello mushrooms, sliced
Olive oil
Bottled or fresh basil pesto
1 French baguette, sliced

Leaf lettuce
Tomato slices
Red onion slices
Mozzarella cheese slices

Brush the mushrooms with olive oil. Cook on a hot grill for 2 to 3 minutes on each side. Spread the pesto on one side of the bread slices. Add lettuce, tomato, onion, cheese and grilled mushrooms to half of the bread slices. Top with the remaining bread slices.

• • • • •

Shiitake Mushroom Napoleons
Serves Eight

Frozen puff pastry sheets
1 pound shiitake mushrooms, sliced
$1/4$ cup butter
$3/4$ cup marsala

$1/2$ cup cream
$1/4$ teaspoon oregano
Salt and pepper to taste
8 ounces Brie or Camembert cheese

Cut the puff pastry into 2x4-inch rectangles and place on a baking sheet. Bake at 350 degrees for 10 minutes or until golden brown. Cool on a wire rack. Sauté the mushrooms in the butter in a skillet; drain. Add the wine. Cook over medium heat until the liquid is reduced by half, stirring frequently. Stir in the cream, oregano, salt and pepper. Cook over medium heat until reduced by half, stirring frequently. Cut the cheese into 8 rectangles. Place 1 piece of baked pastry on each of 8 serving plates. Add 1 slice of cheese and $1/8$ of the mushroom mixture to each. Top with a second piece of pastry.

Olives

A bowl of olives is a great way to begin! Their saltiness is perfect with drinks, and their earthy colors complement a variety of foods. When serving olives, offer your guests a choice of at least two kinds, such as:

Alfonso: black, huge and delicious.

Royal or Victoria: very large, black Greek olives that are cured in olive oil.

Sicilian: small, oval, cracked green Italian olives cured in salt brine; traditionally spiced with red pepper and oregano.

Calabrese: a dull bronze-green olive, more mellow.

Kalamata: large, almond-shaped Greek Olive is purple-black, powerful in flavor; often considered the best of all olives.

Spiced Pecans
Serves Ten

Butter
1 cup sugar
1 teaspoon cinnamon
$^1/_2$ teaspoon salt

$^1/_2$ cup water
$1^1/_2$ teaspoons vanilla extract
$2^1/_2$ cups pecan halves, warmed

Butter the sides of a 2-quart saucepan. Add the sugar, cinnamon, salt and water. Bring the mixture to a boil over medium heat, stirring occasionally. Cook to 234-240 degrees on a candy thermometer, soft-ball stage. Beat until creamy. Add the vanilla and the warmed pecans, mixing well. Spread onto a buttered plate and break into serving pieces. Let stand until cool. Store in an airtight container. Do not refrigerate.

. . . . .

Pickled Olives
Serves Twenty

44 ounces assorted olives
2 cups olive oil
12 cups red wine vinegar
1 cup liquid from green olives
8 cloves of garlic, sliced
2 tablespoons black peppercorns
1 tablespoon crushed red pepper

12 bay leaves
2 teaspoons oregano
2 teaspoons thyme
Grated peel of 1 lemon
Chopped fresh parsley to taste
Sliced onions to taste

Combine the olives, olive oil, red wine vinegar, olive liquid, garlic, peppercorns, red pepper, bay leaves, oregano, thyme, lemon peel, parsley and onions in a large container; mix well. Let stand, covered, for 1 week, stirring occasionally.

COCKTAIL PARTY

SPINACH EMPANADAS
Makes Sixty

16 ounces cream cheese, softened
$^1/_4$ cup butter or margarine
$2^1/_2$ cups flour
1 teaspoon salt
4 to 5 slices bacon
$^1/_4$ cup finely chopped onion
3 cloves of garlic, minced
6 to 8 ounces cottage cheese or feta cheese
1 (10-ounce) package frozen chopped spinach, thawed, drained
$^1/_4$ teaspoon pepper
$^1/_8$ teaspoon nutmeg
1 egg, beaten

Combine the cream cheese and butter in a mixer bowl, beating until smooth. Add the flour and salt gradually, mixing well after each addition. Knead the dough lightly by hand. Store, covered with plastic wrap, in the refrigerator for 3 hours. Cook the bacon in a skillet until crisp; drain, reserving 1 tablespoon bacon drippings. Crumble the bacon. Cook the onion and garlic in the reserved bacon drippings in a skillet until soft. Stir in the bacon, cottage cheese, spinach, pepper and nutmeg. Allow the mixture to cool. Roll out the cream cheese pastry on a lightly floured surface until $^1/_8$-inch thick. Cut with a 3-inch biscuit cutter. Spoon 1 teaspoon of the spinach mixture onto half of each circle. Moisten the edge of the pastry with the egg and fold to enclose the filling, sealing the edge with a fork. Place on an ungreased baking sheet. Brush the tops with the egg and cut a small vent with a fork. Bake at 450 degrees for 10 to 12 minutes or until golden brown. May freeze for later use. Serve with salsa.

FAVORITE SANDWICH COMBINATIONS

Try these tempting variations:
   Sweet butter, watercress leaves, a thin slice of cucumber, salt and pepper, served as a closed sandwich on white bread rounds.
   Whipped cream cheese, smoked salmon and a sprig of dill, served open-face on wheat bread rounds.
   Basil-Parmesan mayonnaise and a thin slice of tomato, served as a closed sandwich on white bread rounds.

COCKTAIL CROISSANTS
Serves Six

12 miniature croissants
8 ounces garlic-herb soft cream
   cheese

³/₄ pound cooked turkey, thinly
   sliced
1 package alfalfa sprouts

Cut the croissants into halves. Spread the cream cheese on the cut sides. Layer 2 or 3 slices of turkey and some of the sprouts on the bottom halves of the croissants. Replace the tops.

• • • • •

VEGETABLE SANDWICH SPREAD
Serves Twelve

1 small cucumber, peeled
Salt to taste
2 to 3 small carrots, grated
1 small onion, finely chopped

3 tablespoons mayonnaise
Pepper to taste
8 ounces cream cheese, softened
12 thin slices bread

Chop or grate the cucumber; sprinkle with salt. Let stand for several minutes. Drain the cucumber. Combine the cucumber, carrots and onion in a bowl and mix well. Drain the vegetables. Combine the vegetables, mayonnaise, salt, pepper and cream cheese in a bowl and mix well. Spread on 6 slices of bread. Top with the remaining bread. Cut into halves.

Beef Teriyaki
Serves Six

½ cup soy sauce
1 tablespoon sugar
¼ cup sherry or 7-Up beverage
1 clove of garlic, minced

½ teaspoon finely chopped ginger
1 pound (¼-inch thick) flank steak,
  cut into strips

Combine the soy sauce, sugar, sherry, garlic and ginger in a bowl and mix well.
Place the beef strips in a shallow bowl. Pour the soy sauce mixture over the beef.
Marinate, covered, in the refrigerator for 1 to 2 hours. Thread the beef onto
skewers. Grill about 4 inches from the hot coals for 2 to 3 minutes on each side
or cook under a broiler. Serve hot.

· · · · ·

Blackened Pork Loin Roast
Serves Twenty

3 tablespoons paprika
½ teaspoon cayenne pepper
2 cloves of garlic, minced
2 teaspoons oregano
2 teaspoons thyme
½ teaspoon salt

½ teaspoon white pepper
½ teaspoon cumin
¼ teaspoon nutmeg
2 pounds boneless pork loin
1 teaspoon olive oil

Combine the paprika, cayenne pepper, garlic, oregano, thyme, salt, white pepper,
cumin and nutmeg in a small bowl and mix well. Rub the surface of the pork
with the olive oil. Rub the seasoning mixture over the pork. Place the pork in a
shallow roasting pan. Bake at 350 degrees for 1 hour. Let stand for 5 to 10
minutes before slicing. Cut into very thin slices for cocktail sandwiches.

MUSTARD SAUCE

1 tablespoon dry mustard
$^{1}/_{4}$ cup Dijon mustard
2 tablespoons sugar
2 tablespoons apple cider
   vinegar
$^{1}/_{2}$ teaspoon salt
4 egg yolks, beaten
1 cup plain yogurt or heavy
   cream

Combine the dry mustard,
Dijon mustard, sugar, vinegar,
salt and egg yolks in a double
boiler. Cook over boiling
water until thickened, stirring
constantly. Remove from the
heat. Stir in the yogurt.

GRILLED PORK TENDERLOIN WITH MUSTARD SAUCE

Serves Twenty

$^{1}/_{2}$ cup teriyaki sauce
$^{1}/_{4}$ cup plus 2 tablespoons soy sauce
1 (5-pound) pork loin roast

Mustard Sauce (at left)
Walnut Bread (page 82)

Combine the teriyaki sauce and soy sauce in a bowl and mix well. Place the
pork roast in a shallow bowl. Pour the marinade over the pork. Marinate,
covered, in the refrigerator for 8 to 10 hours, turning occasionally. Remove from
the marinade. Grill over hot coals to sear the pork. Reduce the heat. Cook the
pork to 150 degrees on a meat thermometer. Cut into thin slices and serve with
Mustard Sauce on thinly sliced Walnut Bread.

• • • • •

PORK TENDERLOIN

Serves Sixteen

1 cup soy sauce
2 tablespoons sugar
1 tablespoon dried onion flakes

$^{1}/_{4}$ cup sesame seeds
2 tablespoons vegetable oil
4 pounds pork tenderloin

Combine the soy sauce, sugar, onion flakes, sesame seeds and oil in a bowl
and mix well. Place the pork in a roasting pan. Pour the marinade over the pork.
Marinate, covered, in the refrigerator for 8 to 10 hours, turning occasionally.
Bake, covered, at 350 degrees for 1$^{1}/_{2}$ hours. Remove the cover. Bake at 350
degrees for 30 minutes longer.

John's Venison Marinade

$^{1}/_{2}$ **cup vegetable oil**
$^{3}/_{4}$ **cup soy sauce**
$^{1}/_{2}$ **vinegar**
$^{1}/_{3}$ **cup lemon juice**
$^{1}/_{4}$ **cup Worcestershire sauce**
2 tablespoons dry mustard
1 teaspoon pepper
2 teaspoons chopped fresh
  parsley

Combine the oil, soy sauce, vinegar, lemon juice, Worcestershire sauce, dry mustard, pepper and parsley in a bowl and mix well. Place the venison in a shallow dish. Pour the marinade over the venison. Marinate, covered, in the refrigerator for at least 48 hours before cooking. May also use to marinate pork tenderloin.

Unbelievable Marinated Grilled Venison
Serves Variable Amount

2 cups safflower oil
1 cup apple cider vinegar
$^{3}/_{4}$ **cup soy sauce**
$^{1}/_{4}$ **cup Worcestershire sauce**
Venison strips, sinew removed

Pepper to taste
Ground ginger to taste
Powdered or granulated garlic
  to taste
Celery seeds to taste

Combine the safflower oil, vinegar, soy sauce and Worcestershire sauce in a bowl and mix well. Sprinkle the venison with pepper, ginger, garlic and celery seeds. Pierce both sides of the venison with a fork at $^{1}/_{4}$-inch intervals. Place venison in a shallow bowl. Pour the oil marinade over the venison. Marinate, covered, in the refrigerator for several hours, turning occasionally. Grill over hot coals for 4 minutes, turning 1 time. Do not overcook.

. . . . .

Lamboll Street Torte
Serves Ten

1 (4-ounce) package goat cheese
  with herbs
8 ounces cream cheese, softened
$^{1}/_{4}$ **cup butter, softened (optional)**
1 cup red wine
$^{1}/_{4}$ **cup olive oil**

3 shallots, finely chopped
1 teaspoon basil
1 package sun-dried tomatoes,
  chopped
Pesto
Toasted pine nuts

Combine the goat cheese, cream cheese and butter in a bowl and mix well. Spread into a circle on a round serving platter. Chill, covered, for 8 to 10 hours. Combine the red wine, olive oil, shallots and basil in a bowl and mix well. Add the sun-dried tomatoes. Marinate, covered, in the refrigerator for 8 to 10 hours. Drain the tomatoes. Spread the pesto over the top of the cheese mixture. Arrange the tomatoes and pine nuts over the pesto. Serve with French bread.

CRAB CROSTINI
Serves Eight

8 ounces lump crab meat
¹/₂ cup finely chopped red bell
  pepper
2 tablespoons plus 2 teaspoons
  reduced-calorie mayonnaise
2 tablespoons chopped fresh parsley
1 tablespoon chopped fresh chives

1 tablespoon fresh lime juice
1 tablespoon Dijon mustard
2 teaspoons grated Parmesan cheese
4 to 5 drops hot pepper sauce
4 ounces Italian bread, cut into 16
  slices

Remove the cartilage from the crab meat. Combine the red pepper, mayonnaise, parsley, chives, lime juice, Dijon mustard, Parmesan cheese and hot pepper sauce in a bowl and mix well. Add the crab meat and mix well. Spread 1 tablespoon of the crab mixture on each slice of bread. Place on a broiler pan. Broil in a preheated broiler for 5 to 6 minutes or until light brown. May store the crab mixture, covered, in the refrigerator for several hours before using. May substitute 1 teaspoon finely chopped green onion tops for the chives.

■ ■ ■ ■ ■

FOLLY BEACH CRAB CANAPÉS
Makes Forty-Eight

¹/₄ cup butter, softened
1 tablespoon mayonnaise
¹/₄ teaspoon garlic salt
1 (8-ounce) jar Old English cheese
  spread

6 ounces fresh crab meat
6 whole English muffins, split

Combine the butter, mayonnaise, garlic salt and cheese spread in a bowl and mix well. Add the crab meat and mix well. Spread the mixture on the English muffin halves. Cut each muffin half into quarters. Place on a baking sheet. Broil in a preheated broiler for 5 minutes or until light brown and crisp. May freeze in an airtight container before baking. Broil frozen canapés for 6 to 7 minutes.

Chef Ramona Measom's Mussels In Beer

Serves Variable Amount

4 leeks (white part only), thinly sliced
1 bunch green onions, sliced
1 (6-pack) beer
1 tablespoon red pepper flakes

2 yellow onions, sliced vertically
Mussels
$1/2$ cup chopped tomatoes
Cooked pasta

Combine the leeks, green onions, beer and red pepper flakes in a saucepan. Cut the yellow onions into 2-inch strips. Add to the saucepan. Bring to a boil over medium heat. Reduce the heat. Simmer, covered, for 10 minutes, stirring occasionally. Scrub each mussel with a brush under cold running water, scraping off the beards and removing the grit. Heat a large nonstick skillet over medium heat until very hot. Add a handful of mussels at a time, 1 cup beer broth and $1/2$ cup chopped tomatoes. Steam, covered, removing the mussels as they open. Continue cooking mussels, adding additional beer broth and chopped tomatoes as needed. Serve the mussels over the cooked pasta, topping with the pan juices. May also use this recipe for clams.

. . . . .

Chef Ramona Measom was a surgical technician and upon a move to Charleston decided to pursue her real love: cooking. She is a graduate of Johnson and Wales Culinary Institute and has worked at Louis's Charleston Grill for Louis Osteen, one of America's premier chefs. She is currently working with Chef Louis Osteen in his new restaurant venture.

HOLY-MOLY MUSSELS
Serves Eight

1 cup white wine
1 cup water
1 large onion, coarsely chopped
2 cloves of garlic, finely chopped

1 large tomato, coarsely chopped
10 tiny carrots or 2 large carrots, peeled, coarsely chopped
2 pounds mussels

Combine the wine, water, onion, garlic, tomato and carrots in a bowl and mix well. Let stand, covered, at room temperature for several hours. Pour into a large saucepan. Bring to a boil over medium heat. Reduce heat and simmer for up to 10 minutes. Scrub each mussel with a brush under cold running water, scraping off the beards and removing the grit. Add the mussels to the saucepan. Steam, covered, for 1 minute. Stir the mussels up from the bottom. Steam, covered, for 1 minute longer. Remove the opened mussels. Steam, covered, for 1 minute longer if some mussels still are not open. Remove the opened mussels and discard any unopened mussels. Serve immediately. Allow 1/4 pound mussels per person as an appetizer or 1 pound per person for a main dish.

• • • • •

OYSTERS ROCKEFELLER
Makes Eighteen

1/4 cup chopped celery
1/4 cup chopped green onions
2 tablespoons chopped parsley
1/4 cup butter
1 (10-ounce) package frozen chopped spinach, thawed, drained

1 tablespoon anisette liqueur
1/4 teaspoon salt
1 pint shucked oysters
1/4 cup dry bread crumbs
1 tablespoon melted butter

Sauté the celery, onions and parsley in 1/4 cup butter in a skillet for 5 minutes. Combine the sautéed vegetables, spinach, anisette and salt in a blender container. Process until the spinach is puréed. Place 18 baking shells on a bed of rock salt in a baking pan. Spoon the spinach mixture evenly into the baking shells. Add the oysters. Sprinkle with the bread crumbs and drizzle with the melted butter. Bake at 450 degrees for 10 minutes.

COOPER RIVER PICKLED SHRIMP

Serves Twenty

1 medium onion, sliced
1 medium bell pepper, cut
  into strips
2 large carrots, julienned
3 teaspoons celery seeds
3 or 4 bay leaves
2 bottles zesty Italian
  dressing
Salt and pepper to taste
3 pounds shrimp, cooked,
  peeled, deveined

Separate the onion slices into rings. Combine the onion, bell pepper, carrots, celery seeds, bay leaves, Italian dressing, salt and pepper in a glass bowl and mix well. Stir in the shrimp. Chill, covered, in the refrigerator for at least 24 hours before serving.

OYSTERS IN CHAMPAGNE CREAM SAUCE

Serves Eight

4 parsley sprigs
1 bay leaf
1/2 teaspoon fresh thyme leaves
13/4 cup Champagne
4 shallots, chopped
1/8 teaspoon salt
Freshly ground white pepper
8 ounces fresh mushrooms, thinly
  sliced
11/2 pounds shucked oysters
1 cup whipping cream
2 egg yolks, at room temperature
3 tablespoons flour
2 tablespoons butter, softened
1 tablespoon fresh lemon juice
2/3 cup coarse dry bread crumbs
1/4 cup melted butter

Tie the parsley, bay leaf and thyme in cheesecloth and place in a large heavy saucepan. Add the Champagne, shallots, salt and white pepper. Bring to a boil over medium heat. Reduce the heat. Simmer for 5 minutes. Add the mushrooms. Simmer for 5 minutes or just until the mushrooms are tender, stirring occasionally. Drain the oysters, reserving the liquid. Add the oysters to the saucepan, adding enough of the reserved liquid to cover. Simmer for 4 minutes or just until the edges of the oysters begin to curl. Remove the mushrooms and oysters with a slotted spoon and place in a bowl. Boil the liquid until reduced to 11/4 cups. Strain into another saucepan. Beat the whipping cream and egg yolks together in a bowl. Mix the flour and softened butter together in a bowl until well blended. Place the saucepan with the reduced liquid over low heat. Add the cream mixture in a fine stream, whisking until blended. Add enough of the flour mixture to thicken the sauce, stirring constantly. Add the lemon juice. Remove from the heat. Stir in the mushrooms and oysters. Spoon the mixture into 8 gratin dishes. Mix the bread crumbs with the remaining melted butter in a bowl. Sprinkle over the oysters. Broil under a preheated broiler until the oysters are heated through and the bread crumbs are brown.

Legare Street Shrimp Rémoulade
Serves Ten

1/4 cup white vinegar
1/4 cup lemon juice
1/4 cup prepared mustard
1/4 cup prepared horseradish
2 tablespoons catsup
2 teaspoons salt
1 teaspoon pepper

1 cup vegetable oil
1/2 cup finely chopped celery
1/2 cup finely chopped onion
1 tablespoon small capers
Boston lettuce leaves
3 pounds medium shrimp, cooked, peeled, deveined, chilled

Combine the vinegar, lemon juice, mustard, horseradish, catsup, salt and pepper in a bowl and mix well. Add the oil in a fine stream, beating rapidly. Stir in the celery, onion and capers. Line 10 serving plates with lettuce. Spoon shrimp onto the lettuce and drizzle the dressing over the top. Garnish with calamata olives.

• • • • •

Red House Plantation Pickled Shrimp
Serves Forty

1 quart white vinegar
1 pint vegetable oil
1 quart catsup
Hot pepper sauce to taste
Coarsely ground pepper to taste
1 pound small onions, sliced

2 (16-ounce) jars boiled onions, drained
6 bell peppers, cut into rings
10 pounds shrimp, cooked, peeled, deveined

Combine the vinegar, oil, catsup, hot pepper sauce and pepper in a bowl and mix well. Separate the onion slices into rings. Add onion rings, boiled onions and bell peppers to the vinegar mixture and mix well. Stir in the shrimp. Spoon the mixture into jars and seal with 2-piece lids or store in one large container. Store in the refrigerator for 2 weeks before serving, shaking the jars occasionally. These are given as Christmas gifts and are eagerly awaited by friends.

LOWCOUNTRY SAUTÉED SHRIMP
Serves Eight

2 to 4 cloves of garlic, minced
$^{1}/_{2}$ cup butter
2 pounds uncooked peeled shrimp
2 to 3 tablespoons flour

$^{1}/_{4}$ teaspoon mace
$^{1}/_{4}$ cup chopped parsley
Salt and pepper to taste

Sauté the garlic in 1 tablespoon of the butter in a heavy covered skillet for 30 seconds. Add the shrimp. Cook for 30 seconds and pour off the liquid into a bowl. Continue to cook for 30 seconds at a time, pouring off the liquid and reserving in a bowl. Add the remaining butter when there is a minimal amount of liquid forming in the skillet. Add the flour and cook for 1 minute, stirring to blend and coat the shrimp. Add the reserved shrimp liquid, mace and water if needed. Cook until thickened, stirring constantly. Add the parsley, salt and pepper. Serve as an appetizer or over grits as a main dish.

• • • • •

ARTICHOKE DIP
Serves Sixteen

5 slices bacon
1 onion, chopped
1 clove of garlic, minced
$^{1}/_{2}$ cup mayonnaise
8 ounces cream cheese, softened

8 ounces Swiss cheese, shredded
2 (14-ounce) cans artichoke hearts, drained
Parmesan cheese
Pita bread

Fry the bacon in a skillet until crisp. Remove the bacon to a paper towel to drain. Sauté the onion and garlic in the pan drippings just until soft; remove with a slotted spoon. Combine the mayonnaise, cream cheese and Swiss cheese in a bowl and mix well. Chop the artichokes and add to the cheese mixture. Add the onion and garlic and mix well. Spoon into a round baking dish. Sprinkle with Parmesan cheese. Crumble the bacon and sprinkle over the top. Bake at 350 degrees for 30 minutes. Cut the pita bread into wedges and serve with the dip.

BLACK-EYED PEA DIP
Serves Sixteen

2 (15-ounce) cans black-eyed peas
2 to 3 tablespoons chopped fresh
  cilantro

3 to 4 green onions, chopped
Zesty Italian salad dressing

Rinse and drain the black-eyed peas. Combine the black-eyed peas, cilantro and onions in a bowl and mix well. Add enough salad dressing to the mixture to cover. Marinate, covered, in the refrigerator for 24 hours before serving. Drain and serve with corn chips or tortilla chips.

■ ■ ■ ■ ■

FIESTA SALSA
Serves Twenty

1 (7-ounce) can Shoe Peg corn,
  drained
1 (15-ounce) can black beans,
  drained

1 (16-ounce) jar medium salsa
1/4 cup chopped green bell pepper
Cumin to taste
Garlic salt to taste

Combine the corn, black beans, salsa, green pepper, cumin and garlic salt in a bowl and mix well. Pour into a serving bowl. Chill, covered, until serving time. Serve with tortilla chips.

Salsa And Black Bean Dip
Serves Eight

1 (15-ounce) can black beans,
   drained
1/2 cup chopped green onions

1 to 2 cups thick and chunky salsa
4 to 6 slices crisp-cooked bacon,
   crumbled

Combine the black beans, onions, salsa and bacon in a bowl and mix well. Spoon into a serving bowl. Chill, covered, for 1 to 2 hours before serving. Serve with baked tortilla chips.

• • • • •

Caponata
Serves Ten

1 large onion, finely chopped
2 cloves of garlic, minced
2 medium bell peppers, finely
   chopped
1/2 cup olive oil
3 medium eggplants, chopped
1 (10-ounce) can tomatoes with
   green chiles

1 tablespoon sugar
1/2 cup catsup
1 tablespoon Worcestershire sauce
2 1/2 teaspoons salt
3 tablespoons dry white wine
1 (2-ounce) jar capers, drained

Sauté the onion, garlic and bell peppers in the olive oil in a large skillet for 5 minutes. Add the eggplants. Sauté for 20 minutes. Add the tomatoes with green chiles, sugar, catsup, Worcestershire sauce, salt, wine and capers and mix well. Simmer for 30 to 40 minutes, stirring occasionally. Pour into a serving bowl. Chill, covered, in the refrigerator. Serve cold or at room temperature with crackers.

Harbor Dip
Serves Twenty

1 (14-ounce) can artichoke hearts, drained
1 (6-ounce) jar marinated artichoke hearts, drained
8 ounces fresh mushrooms, sautéed
1 (4-ounce) can black olives, drained

$^1/_3$ cup (or more) chopped jalapeños
1 cup mayonnaise
1 cup shredded fresh Parmesan cheese
1 (8-ounce) jar salsa

Combine the artichokes, mushrooms, olives and jalapeños in a food processor container. Process until finely chopped. Combine the chopped vegetables, mayonnaise, Parmesan cheese and salsa in a bowl and mix well. Pour into an ovenproof serving dish. Bake at 350 degrees until heated through. Serve with corn chips. May substitute one 6-ounce can mushrooms for the fresh mushrooms.

▪ ▪ ▪ ▪ ▪

Hot Tortilla Chip Dip
Serves Ten

16 ounces cream cheese, softened
1 avocado, peeled, cut into cubes
1 (12-ounce) jar salsa
$^1/_2$ cup sliced black olives

$1^1/_2$ cups shredded Cheddar cheese
Chopped green onions to taste
Chopped jalapeño to taste

Layer the cream cheese, avocado, salsa, olives, cheese, onions and jalapeño in a 9x12-inch baking dish. Bake at 350 degrees for 15 minutes. Serve with tortilla chips.

Hummus With Roasted Red Pepper

Serves Eight

1 red bell pepper
1 (16-ounce) can chick-peas
3 cloves of garlic, peeled

Juice of 2 lemons
1 tablespoon tahini
1/2 cup extra-virgin olive oil

Broil the red pepper under a hot broiler until blackened on all sides, turning with tongs. Enclose in a brown paper bag for 20 to 30 minutes or until the skin is easily peeled. Remove the seeds and ribs and finely chop the pepper. Drain half the liquid from the chick-peas. Combine the chick-peas, remaining liquid, garlic, lemons and tahini in a food processor. Process until finely chopped. Add the oil in a fine stream, processing constantly until mixture is smooth. Pour into a serving bowl. Fold in pepper gently. Serve with pita chips or toasted pita bread. This is beautiful served in a hollowed-out red bell pepper.

• • • • •

Million Dollar Dip

Serves Eight

16 ounces sharp Cheddar cheese,
  shredded
1 pound crisp-cooked bacon,
  crumbled
6 green onions, finely chopped

2 (3-ounce) packages sliced
  almonds
Salt and pepper to taste
1 cup (about) mayonnaise

Combine the cheese, bacon, onions, almonds, salt and pepper in a bowl and mix well. Add just enough mayonnaise to bind the ingredients together. Spoon into a serving bowl. Chill, covered, for at least 1 hour. Let stand at room temperature for 30 minutes before serving. Serve with Triscuits or thinly sliced baguette.

WADMALAW SWEET ONIONS

The strength of an onion depends on the variety and its origin; the warmer the climate, the sweeter the onion. Located south of Charleston is a rural island named Wadmalaw Island. It is a haven for the best fresh fruits and vegetables. The Wadmalaw Sweet Onion is grown there and is a local favorite. It is compared to the well known Vidalia Onion grown further south.

VIDALIA ONION DIP
Serves Eight

1 cup chopped Vidalia onion or other sweet onion
1 cup shredded Cheddar cheese

1/2 cup mayonnaise
4 drops hot pepper sauce

Combine the onion, cheese, mayonnaise and hot pepper sauce in a bowl and mix well. Spoon into a shallow 6x9-inch baking dish. Bake at 350 degrees for 30 to 40 minutes or until the edges are brown. Serve hot with corn chips or crackers.

• • • • •

PUMPKIN DIP
Serves Six

2 cups sifted confectioners' sugar
8 ounces cream cheese, softened
1 teaspoon cinnamon
1/2 teaspoon ginger

1 (15-ounce) can pumpkin pie filling
Gingersnap cookies

Combine the confectioners' sugar and cream cheese in a bowl and mix well. Add the cinnamon, ginger and pumpkin pie filling and mix well. Spoon into a serving bowl. Chill, covered, until serving time. Serve with gingersnap cookies. May make ahead and freeze.

Fresh Tomato Salsa
Serves Twelve

4 large tomatoes, coarsely
  chopped
4 green onions and tops, coarsely
  chopped
1/2 green bell pepper, coarsely
  chopped
1/2 yellow or orange bell pepper,
  coarsely chopped

15 to 20 Greek black olives, cut into
  halves
1/4 cup olive oil
Salt and pepper to taste
Fresh homemade bread

Combine the tomatoes, onions and tops, bell peppers, olives and olive oil in a bowl and mix well. Season with salt and pepper. Spread on fresh homemade bread just before serving.

■　■　■　■　■

Tomato Topping
Serves Ten

3 fresh tomatoes, finely chopped
1/2 yellow bell pepper, coarsely
  chopped
1/2 orange or green bell pepper,
  coarsely chopped

1 clove of garlic, minced
4 green onions and tops, chopped
1/4 cup Greek pitted black olives,
  chopped
Salt and pepper to taste

Combine the tomatoes, bell peppers, garlic, onions and tops, olives, salt and pepper in a bowl, sprinkling lightly with salt and heavily with pepper and mix well. Use as a topping on bruschetta, fresh bread or pizza, or as a dip for nacho chips.

JALAPEÑO TOMATO SALSA
Serves Eight

4 tomatoes, finely chopped
1/2 small red onion or sweet onion,
   finely chopped
2 teaspoons lime juice

Salt to taste
4 to 8 jalapeño slices, minced
1/4 cup chopped fresh cilantro

Combine the tomatoes, onion, lime juice and salt in a bowl and mix well. Stir in the jalapeño and cilantro. Pour into a serving bowl. Chill, covered, for 2 to 4 hours before serving. Serve with tortilla chips. May substitute 1 tablespoon dried cilantro for the fresh cilantro.

■ ■ ■ ■ ■

MARINATED GOAT CHEESE
Serves Variable Amount

1 clove of garlic, minced
2 tablespoons chopped fresh parsley
2 tablespoons chopped chives
1/2 teaspoon basil
1/2 teaspoon thyme

1/2 teaspoon black pepper
1 small bay leaf
1 cup olive oil, heated
Goat cheese

Combine the garlic, parsley, chives, basil, thyme, pepper and bay leaf in a bowl and mix well. Pour hot oil over the herbs. Be sure the oil is not hot enough to burn the herbs. Place the cheese in a shallow bowl. Pour the marinade over the cheese. Marinate, covered, in the refrigerator for 3 days, turning occasionally. Serve on a bed of fresh herbs. Garnish with roasted red bell peppers and marinated olives. Serve with crusty French bread.

WINE PUNCH SLUSH

Serves Twelve

1 (16-ounce) can frozen pink
   lemonade concentrate
3 cans water
1¹/₂ bottles rosé wine

Combine the pink lemonade
concentrate, water and wine in
a bowl and mix well. Pour into
a freezer container. Freeze,
covered, until slushy.

SPICED TOMATO SPREAD

Makes Six (One-Cup) Jars

2¹/₄ pounds tomatoes, peeled and
   chopped
1¹/₂ teaspoons grated lemon peel
¹/₄ cup fresh lemon juice
¹/₂ teaspoon allspice

¹/₂ teaspoon cinnamon
¹/₄ teaspoon ground cloves
1 package fruit pectin
¹/₂ teaspoon butter or margarine
4¹/₂ cups sugar

Place the tomatoes in a saucepan. Bring to a boil over medium heat. Reduce
the heat. Simmer, covered, over low heat for 10 minutes, stirring occasionally.
Measure 3 cups of the tomatoes into a 6 to 8-quart saucepan. Stir in the lemon
peel, lemon juice, allspice, cinnamon, cloves, fruit pectin and butter. Bring to a
full rolling boil over high heat, stirring constantly. Stir in all the sugar at once.
Return to a full rolling boil and cook for exactly 1 minute, stirring constantly.
Remove from the heat. Skim off any foam with a metal spoon. Ladle into hot,
sterilized jars, leaving ¹/₂-inch head space. Wipe the jar rims and threads. Seal
with 2-piece lids. Invert the jars for 5 minutes; turn upright and check the seals.

• • • • •

CLAM DIP

Serves Six

2 (4-ounce) cans minced clams
¹/₂ green bell pepper, minced
¹/₂ onion, minced
¹/₂ cup melted butter or margarine
1 to 2 tablespoons parsley flakes or
   finely chopped fresh parsley

1 teaspoon oregano
¹/₂ to 1 tablespoon Tabasco sauce
³/₄ cup seasoned bread crumbs
¹/₄ cup Parmesan cheese
1 slice American cheese
Paprika

Combine the undrained clams, green pepper, onion, butter, parsley flakes,
oregano, Tabasco sauce, bread crumbs and Parmesan cheese in a bowl and mix
well. Spoon into a buttered 1-quart baking dish. Place the American cheese slice
on the top. Sprinkle with paprika. Bake at 350 degrees for 20 to 30 minutes or
until hot and bubbly. Serve with corn chips. May be frozen before baking.

CRAB MORNAY DIP
Serves Sixteen

1 loaf thinly sliced white bread
1/2 cup melted butter
1 small bunch green onions, chopped
1/2 cup finely chopped fresh parsley
1/2 cup butter
2 tablespoons flour

1 1/2 cups half-and-half
12 ounces Swiss cheese, shredded
Ground red pepper to taste
Hot pepper sauce to taste
1 pound fresh lump crab meat
1 tablespoon dry sherry

Cut the bread slices into rounds with a 2-inch biscuit cutter. Brush with the melted butter and press buttered-side-down into miniature muffin cups. Bake at 350 degrees until the croustades are brown and toasty. Sauté the onions and parsley in the butter in a skillet for 1 minute. Blend in the flour. Cook for 2 minutes, stirring constantly. Remove from the heat. Whisk in the half-and-half. Cook over low heat while stirring in the cheese, pepper and hot pepper sauce. Stir in the crab and sherry shortly before serving. Serve hot in a chafing dish with croustades. Croustades may be made ahead, frozen and reheated for 5 minutes.

■ ■ ■ ■ ■

MT. PLEASANT CRAB CAKES
Serves Six

1 pound crab meat
1 cup mayonnaise
1 egg white
12 crushed crackers
1 teaspoon celery seeds

1/4 teaspoon lemon juice
Salt, pepper and cayenne pepper to taste
Italian bread crumbs
Butter for frying

Combine the crab meat, mayonnaise, egg white, cracker crumbs, celery seeds, lemon juice, salt, pepper and cayenne pepper in a bowl and mix well. Shape into patties. Dip in the Italian bread crumbs to coat. Fry in butter in a skillet until crisp and brown. Keep warm on a serving platter in a 200-degree oven. May freeze before frying.

DILLY SHRIMP DIP
Serves Eight

16 ounces cream cheese, softened
1/4 cup half-and-half
2 green onions, finely chopped
1 teaspoon hot pepper sauce

1 teaspoon dillweed
Salt to taste
1 cup chopped deveined peeled
   cooked shrimp

Combine the cream cheese, half-and-half, onions, hot pepper sauce, dillweed and salt in a bowl and mix well. Stir in the shrimp. Chill, covered, until serving time. Serve with thin wheat crackers.

▪ ▪ ▪ ▪ ▪

KIAWAH SHRIMP BUTTER
Serves Eight

3/4 cup butter, softened
8 ounces cream cheese, softened
1 tablespoon finely minced onion
Juice of 1/2 lemon

1/4 cup mayonnaise
1 pound small shrimp, cooked,
   peeled, deveined, minced

Combine the butter, cream cheese, onion, lemon juice, mayonnaise and shrimp in a blender container or food processor. Process until well mixed. Press into a mold sprayed with nonstick cooking spray. Chill, covered, for 8 to 10 hours. Unmold onto a serving plate. May substitute 2 cans of shrimp, rinsed and drained, for the fresh shrimp. Will keep well for several days in the refrigerator or may be frozen.

THE HEYWARD-WASHINGTON HOUSE KITCHEN

Outbuildings, in the yards of Charleston houses, served important functions. They were used as kitchens, wash kitchens, stables, carriage houses, servants' quarters, etc. The kitchen of the Heyward-Washington House, circa 1772, at 87 Church Street is typical of such facilities. The kitchen was in a building separate from the main house to confine danger of fire, but also to keep heat and cooking odors out of the main residence.

Cooking was done in the oversized fireplace using a variety of pots, pans, and implements. It was primitive compared with twentieth-century kitchens, but quite elaborate meals were produced. Josiah Quincy, a visitor from Boston in the 1770s, remarked on the sumptuous life pattern of the Charleston aristocracy, including their sophisticated diet.

Meals prepared in this kitchen would have been enjoyed not only by Daniel Heyward, the wealthy rice planter who built the mansion and its outbuildings, but also by his son Thomas Heyward, a signer of the Declaration of Independence. President George Washington stayed at the address when he visited Charleston on his official tour of the southern states in 1791.

The Heyward-Washington House, along with its outbuildings and garden, is operated as a house museum by the Charleston Museum.

Soups

Soups

WINE VINEGAR

Pass a cruet of wine vinegar when serving bean soup. A teaspoon or two really helps perk up the flavor.

BLACK BEAN SOUP
Serves Six

2 cups dry black beans
3¹/₂ to 4 cups water
2 to 3 (14-ounce) cans chicken stock
1 onion, chopped
3 cloves of garlic, minced
1 carrot, chopped
1 rib of celery, chopped
1 tablespoon olive oil
1¹/₂ to 2 teaspoons cumin

1 teaspoon coriander
¹/₂ cup freshly squeezed orange juice
Sections of 2 oranges
2 tablespoons dry sherry
¹/₂ teaspoon freshly ground black pepper
¹/₄ teaspoon red pepper
Juice of 1 lemon
Salt to taste

Soak the beans in 3¹/₂ to 4 cups water in a large container for 8 to 12 hours; drain. Place the beans and chicken stock in a large stockpot. Bring to a boil over medium heat. Cover and reduce the heat. Sauté the onion, garlic, carrot and celery in the olive oil in a skillet for several minutes. Add the cumin and coriander and a small amount of water. Steam the vegetables for several minutes or until soft. Add to the beans. Add the orange juice, orange sections, sherry, black and red pepper, lemon juice and salt and stir gently. Simmer for 1¹/₂ to 2 hours or until the beans are tender, stirring occasionally and adding water or chicken stock if needed. May purée some of the beans in a blender for a smoother consistency. Ladle into bowls. Garnish with sour cream or plain yogurt and a sprinkle of finely chopped onions.

CHILLED ZUCCHINI SOUP YEAMAN'S HALL
Serves Four

2 large zucchini, sliced
1 green bell pepper, chopped
1/4 cup finely chopped yellow onion
3 cups chicken stock
1 cup sour cream or plain yogurt

1 tablespoon chopped fresh parsley
1/2 teaspoon chopped fresh dill
Salt and pepper to taste
1/2 cup (or more) chopped zucchini

Reserve 4 slices of the zucchini for garnish. Place the remaining sliced zucchini in a large saucepan. Add the green pepper, onion and chicken stock. Simmer, covered, for 20 minutes. Strain the vegetables, reserving the stock. Combine the vegetables, sour cream, parsley, dill, salt and pepper in a blender container. Process until puréed. Combine the puréed mixture and the reserved stock in a refrigerator container and mix well. Chill, covered, until cold. Ladle into bowls. Add chopped zucchini to give the soup some crunch. Garnish each serving with a reserved slice of zucchini and additional sour cream and dill.

· · · · ·

COMFORT SOUP
Serves Eight

2 tablespoons olive oil
2 medium onions, finely chopped
2 cups chopped carrots
1/4 cup chopped fresh parsley
3 (10-ounce) cans chicken stock
3 to 4 cups coarsely chopped
   potatoes

1/4 cup chopped fresh dill, or
   2 tablespoons dried
Salt and pepper to taste
2 to 3 cups shredded Cheddar
   cheese

Heat the olive oil in a large stockpot over low heat. Add the onions and carrots. Cook, covered, for 20 to 25 minutes or until tender. Add the parsley, chicken stock and potatoes. Bring to a boil over medium heat. Reduce the heat. Simmer, covered, for 30 minutes or until the potatoes are tender. Stir in the dill, salt and pepper. Remove from the heat and let stand, covered, for 5 minutes. Place over low heat. Stir in the cheese gradually. Serve immediately. May add cheese to the soup after ladling into bowls and microwave until cheese is melted.

SUMMER DINNER ON THE PIAZZA

GAZPACHO BLANCA
Serves Six

3 medium cucumbers, peeled
3 cups chicken broth
3 tablespoons white vinegar
2 cups sour cream
1 cup plain yogurt
2 teaspoons salt

2 cloves of garlic, minced
Chopped tomato
3/4 cup chopped almonds, toasted
1/2 cup sliced scallions
1/4 cup chopped fresh parsley

Slice the cucumbers lengthwise into halves; remove the seeds and coarsely chop the cucumbers. Combine the cucumbers and chicken broth in a blender or food processor container. Process until of the desired consistency. Pour into a bowl. Process the vinegar, sour cream, yogurt, salt and garlic in the blender until well mixed. Add to the cucumber mixture and stir just until mixed. Chill, covered, for 2 to 3 hours. Stir again and ladle into chilled bowls. Serve the tomato, almonds, scallions and parsley in separate bowls and let your guests choose their own toppings.

▪ ▪ ▪ ▪ ▪

"STOLEN" GAZPACHO
Serves Ten

7 medium tomatoes, chopped
1 cucumber, chopped
1/2 green bell pepper, chopped
1 large carrot, chopped
1 small onion, chopped, or
    5 green onions with tops,
    chopped
1/2 tablespoon chopped fresh dill

Salt to taste
1/2 teaspoon pepper
3 to 4 tablespoons chopped fresh
    parsley
1/2 cup oil and vinegar-type salad
    dressing (preferably one made
    and advertised by famous
    handsome male movie star)

Combine the tomatoes, cucumber, green pepper, carrot and onion in a large bowl. Sprinkle with dill, salt, pepper and parsley. Add the dressing and toss gently to mix. Chill, covered, for 8 to 10 hours. Process in a food processor just until vegetables are coarsely ground. Serve garnished with sour cream, nonfat plain yogurt or chopped green bell peppers.

CHILLED CURRIED EGGPLANT SOUP WADMALAW

Serves Six

1¹/₄ pounds Wadmalaw eggplant,
   peeled
¹/₂ cup chopped onion
¹/₄ cup butter

1 tablespoon curry powder
4 cups chicken stock
³/₄ cup heavy cream
Salt and white pepper to taste

Cut the eggplant into ¹/₂-inch cubes. Sauté the onion in the butter in a large
stockpot. Stir in the curry powder. Cook for 2 minutes, stirring constantly. Add
the eggplant and chicken stock. Bring to a boil over medium heat. Reduce the
heat. Simmer for 45 minutes or until the eggplant is tender. Purée the soup in
batches in a blender. Pour into a refrigerator container. Chill, covered, until cold.
Stir in the cream, salt and pepper. Ladle into soup bowls.

▪ ▪ ▪ ▪ ▪

LENTIL STEW

Serves Eight

2 cups dried lentils
6 cups vegetable bouillon or water
1 cup chopped onion
2 teaspoons dried basil
2 ribs celery, chopped
4 carrots, chopped

1 (16-ounce) can stewed tomatoes
1 clove of garlic, minced
4 large potatoes, chopped
Salt and pepper to taste
2 tablespoons vinegar

Rinse the lentils in cold water and drain. Bring the vegetable bouillon to a boil
in a large saucepan over medium heat. Add the lentils gradually. Reduce the
heat. Simmer over low heat for 1 hour, stirring occasionally. Add the onion, basil,
celery, carrots, undrained tomatoes, garlic, potatoes, salt and pepper. Cook for
1 hour or until the lentils and potatoes are tender. Stir in the vinegar. Simmer for
5 minutes longer.

*"It breathes reassurance,
it offers consolation;
after a weary day it promotes
sociability . . . There is
nothing like a bowl of hot soup,
its wisp of aromatic steam
teasing the nostrils
into quivering anticipation."*

The Soup Book
Louis P. De Gouy, 1949

CHEF SCOTT ROARK'S CREAM OF MUSHROOM, ONION AND GARLIC SOUP

Serves Eight

½ large yellow onion, diced
½ cup butter
3 cloves of garlic, finely chopped
1½ pounds mushrooms, rinsed
1 cup flour
2 tablespoons white wine
2 cups chicken stock
2 cups milk

½ teaspoon dried thyme
1 bay leaf
½ teaspoon chicken base, or
  1 chicken bouillon cube
2 cups heavy cream or half-and-half
Salt and white pepper to taste
Sliced green onions

Sauté the onion in 2 tablespoons of the butter in a stockpot until translucent. Add the garlic and sauté just until tender. Chop 1 pound of the mushrooms coarsely in a food processor or by hand. Add to the stockpot and sauté just until tender. Melt the remaining 6 tablespoons butter in a large skillet over low heat. Stir in the flour to make a roux. Cook for 5 minutes over low heat, stirring constantly. Add the wine, chicken stock, milk, thyme, bay leaf and chicken base to the mushroom mixture and mix well. Heat to a simmer, stirring frequently. Stir in the roux. Simmer for 15 minutes, stirring frequently. Slice the remaining ½ pound mushrooms and add to the soup. Remove from the heat. Stir in the cream. Remove and discard the bay leaf. Add the salt and pepper. Ladle into bowls and top with sliced green onions.

▪ ▪ ▪ ▪ ▪

Chef Scott Roark has a BA Degree from Roanoke College and is a graduate of the Culinary Institute of America in New York. He was the owner and chef of the Village Cafe for eight years and is currently Program Coordinator for Culinary Arts at Trident Technical College. Chef Roark says, "All through school, I always worked as a waiter and I think that experience inspired me to become a chef."

TORTILLA SOUP CONDIMENT

Break crispy corn chips atop Tortilla Soup for a different consistency. The chips add a great texture to the Tortilla Soup.

TORTILLA SOUP
Serves Six

1/2 cup chopped onion	1 (10-ounce) can tomato juice
1/2 cup chopped green bell pepper	1 1/2 cups water
2 cloves of garlic, minced	1 teaspoon cumin
1 tablespoon vegetable oil	1/2 cup sliced zucchini
1 (14-ounce) can tomatoes	3 boneless skinless chicken breasts,
1 (4-ounce) can green chiles	cooked, chopped
1/2 cup picante sauce	6 corn tortillas, torn into strips
1 (10-ounce) can beef bouillon	1/2 cup shredded low-fat cheese
1 (10-ounce) can chicken bouillon	

Sauté the onion, green pepper and garlic in the oil in a stockpot just until tender. Add the undrained tomatoes, green chiles, picante sauce, beef bouillon, chicken bouillon, tomato juice, water, cumin, zucchini and chicken. Bring to a boil over medium heat. Reduce the heat. Simmer, covered, for 1 hour. Stir in the tortilla strips. Ladle soup into bowls. Sprinkle with cheese.

• • • • •

SPLENDID SPINACH SOUP
Serves Six

1 (16-ounce) package fresh spinach	1 (14-ounce) can chicken broth
2 tablespoons butter	2 cups milk
1 small onion, finely chopped	1/2 teaspoon salt
3 tablespoons flour	1/2 teaspoon nutmeg

Rinse the spinach and trim the stems. Combine with a small amount of water in a large saucepan. Simmer over low heat until spinach is tender, stirring occasionally; drain. Process in a blender until finely chopped. Melt the butter in the saucepan. Sauté the onion in the butter for 3 minutes. Stir in the flour. Add the chicken broth 1/3 at a time, blending well after each addition. Add the spinach. Cook for 2 minutes. Stir in the milk, salt and nutmeg. Heat to serving temperature. Ladle into bowls. Serve with French bread.

BLACK BEAN CHICKEN CHILI

Serves Eight

4 to 6 boneless skinless chicken
  breasts
1 medium onion, chopped
2 medium red bell peppers,
  chopped
4 cloves of garlic, minced
3 tablespoons olive oil
1/4 cup chili powder

2 teaspoons cumin
1 teaspoon coriander
1 (28-ounce) can tomatoes, chopped
1 cup beer
2 (14-ounce) cans black beans
1/4 to 1/2 package medium-sharp
  cold-pack cheese
Salt to taste

Cut the chicken into 1-inch pieces. Sauté the chicken, onion, red peppers and garlic in the olive oil in a stockpot. Add the chili powder, cumin, coriander, undrained tomatoes and beer. Rinse and drain the black beans. Add to the chili. Simmer, covered, over low heat for 1 hour, stirring occasionally. Stir in the cheese just until melted. Season with salt to taste. Serve immediately.

· · · · ·

TURKEY CHILI

Serves Six

1 to 1 1/2 pounds ground turkey
  breast
1 medium onion, chopped
1 green bell pepper, chopped
1 (16-ounce) can tomatoes, chopped
1 (16-ounce) can dark red
  kidney beans

1 (16-ounce) can Spanish rice
1/2 teaspoon chili powder
1 tablespoon cumin
1 clove of garlic, minced
1 1/2 teaspoons oregano
1 (4-ounce) can green chiles

Brown the ground turkey with the onion and green pepper in a large nonstick skillet, stirring until the ground turkey is crumbly. Add the undrained tomatoes, undrained beans, Spanish rice, chili powder, cumin, garlic, oregano and green chiles. Simmer, covered, for 30 to 45 minutes, stirring frequently. Serve with shredded Cheddar cheese if desired. May substitute ground beef for the ground turkey and 1 teaspoon garlic salt for the garlic.

EASY FAMILY DINNER

Serve one of these hearty chilis with a fresh green salad and crusty bread for an easy family dinner.

Basic Vegetarian Chili
Serves Fourteen

3 (16-ounce) cans red kidney beans, drained
2 cloves of garlic, minced
3 tablespoons olive oil
1 large onion, coarsely chopped
1 large carrot, sliced, or 15 baby carrots, cut lengthwise into halves
1 small yellow squash, sliced
1 small zucchini, sliced
2 ribs celery, finely chopped
1/2 small green bell pepper, finely chopped

1/2 small red or yellow bell pepper, finely chopped
1 (28-ounce) can whole tomatoes
1 (28-ounce) can tomato sauce
1 (12-ounce) can tomato paste
1 envelope chili seasoning mix
1 teaspoon pepper
1 teaspoon basil
1 teaspoon parsley
2 bay leaves
1 to 2 teaspoons chili powder
Salt to taste

Rinse the kidney beans and drain. Sauté the garlic in the olive oil for 1 minute. Add the onion. Sauté until tender. Combine the kidney beans, garlic and onion in a slow cooker or large stockpot. Add the carrot, yellow squash, zucchini, celery, bell peppers, undrained tomatoes, tomato sauce and tomato paste; mix gently. Stir in the chili seasoning mix, pepper, basil, parsley and bay leaves. Cook on High for 3 hours. Turn to Low and cook for 3 to 4 hours longer, stirring occasionally. Remove the bay leaves and discard. Adjust the seasonings. Stir in the chili powder and salt to taste. May cook by simmering in a stockpot over low heat for 3 to 4 hours, stirring frequently. Do not cook at a rapid boil or it will burn.

White Sauce

Melt 3 tablespoons butter in a saucepan over low heat. Stir in 3 tablespoon flour. Cook for several minutes, stirring constantly. Add 2 cups milk gradually, mixing well. Cook until thickened, stirring constantly.

Shrimp Stock

Shells from 1 pound shrimp
2¹/₂ cups cold water
¹/₂ onion, sliced
¹/₂ bay leaf

Combine the shrimp shells, water, onion and bay leaf in a saucepan. Simmer for exactly 20 minutes; strain.

Sweet Bell Pepper Corn Bisque
Serves Four

2¹/₂ cups (or more) frozen sweet bell peppers and onions for stir-fry, thawed
1 tablespoon butter
2 (10-ounce) packages frozen silver queen-style creamed corn, thawed
2 cups medium White Sauce (at left)
2 cups half-and-half

2 to 3 tablespoons dried onion flakes, or 1¹/₂ cups chopped onions
³/₄ teaspoon (or more) sage
¹/₂ teaspoon (or more) thyme
Salt and white pepper to taste
Milk

Sauté the bell peppers and onions in the butter in a skillet until tender. Process in a blender until puréed. Pour into a stockpot. Process the corn in the blender until puréed. Add to the stockpot. Combine the White Sauce, half-and-half, onion flakes, sage, thyme, salt and white pepper in a large bowl and add to the stockpot. Simmer over low heat for 30 minutes or longer, stirring occasionally. Adjust the seasonings and add milk if the soup is too thick. Flavor is especially good the second day.

• • • • •

Shrimp Bisque
Serves Four

1 cup finely chopped onion
2 cloves of garlic, finely chopped
1 tablespoon unsalted butter
2 tablespoons olive oil
1 pound shrimp, peeled, deveined
1¹/₂ tablespoons flour
2 tablespoons Cognac

1¹/₂ cups good white wine
2 tablespoons tomato paste
¹/₄ teaspoon curry powder
¹/₄ teaspoon thyme
¹/₄ teaspoon Hungarian paprika
2 cups Shrimp Stock (at left)
1 cup heavy cream

Sauté the onion and garlic in the butter and olive oil in a stockpot until tender. Add the shrimp. Sauté just until the shrimp turn pink. Sprinkle with the flour. Cook for 1 minute, stirring constantly. Add the Cognac, white wine, tomato paste, curry powder, thyme, paprika and Shrimp Stock and mix well. Simmer over low heat for 10 minutes. Add the cream. Simmer for 15 minutes longer, stirring frequently. Process in batches in a blender until puréed. Return to the stockpot and heat to serving temperature. Garnish with chopped parsley and a swirl of additional cream.

EAST BATTERY

East Battery, one of Charleston's most prestigious residential thoroughfares, was a marshy lowland when the first settlers arrived in 1670. The forerunner of today's High Battery was built in 1755 as part of the city's fortifications—an earthwork extending from Granville Bastion on the site of the present-day Missroon House at 40 East Battery to Broughton's Battery on the site of present-day White Point Gardens. The fortified line continued in use through the American Revolution.

The High Battery has been a popular promenade since the early part of the nineteenth century. The city-owned marshland to the west of the Battery gradually was filled and sold to individuals who built mansions along the thoroughfare. The house in the foreground, left, is 5 East Battery, built circa 1847-1849 by John Ravenel. Ravenel, a member of Charleston's Anglo-Huguenot planting aristocracy, was one of the city's leading maritime merchants and was president of the South Carolina Railroad. His son, Dr. St. Julien Ravenel, was a noted scientist who designed and built the Confederate semi-submersible torpedo boat, the *Little David*. He also led the development of the phosphate industry after the Civil War. Dr. Ravenel's wife, Harriott Horry Rutledge, was a noted author. The property remained in the hands of John Ravenel's descendants until 1953.

Salads

East Battery, Charleston, S. C.

SALADS

Holiday Menu

ASPARAGUS ASPIC
Serves Eight

2 envelopes unflavored gelatin
$^1/_2$ cup hot water
1 cup water
$^1/_2$ cup cider vinegar
$^3/_4$ cup sugar
1 teaspoon salt

2 (11-ounce) cans asparagus pieces,
 drained
$^3/_4$ cup chopped pecans
1 cup finely chopped celery
2 tablespoons grated onion

Soften the gelatin in $^1/_2$ cup hot water in a bowl. Combine 1 cup water, vinegar, sugar and salt in a saucepan. Cook over medium heat until the sugar is dissolved, stirring constantly. Add to the softened gelatin, stirring until the gelatin dissolves. Add the asparagus, pecans, celery and onion and mix well. Pour into a 9-inch square glass dish or a gelatin mold. Chill until firm. Cut into squares. Serve on lettuce-lined salad plates.

• • • • •

MARINATED AVOCADOS
Serves Six

2 cups olive oil
$1^1/_2$ cups lemon juice
$1^1/_2$ cups vinegar
6 cloves of garlic, minced
3 tablespoons salt

1 teaspoon cayenne pepper
1 teaspoon cracked black pepper
1 tablespoon dry mustard
6 avocados, sliced

Combine the olive oil, lemon juice, vinegar, garlic, salt, cayenne pepper, cracked pepper and mustard in a bowl and mix well. Pour the marinade over the avocado slices.

BOK CHOY SALAD
Serves Twelve

3 packages ramen noodles
2 tablespoons sesame seeds
3 tablespoons butter
1/2 pound fresh mushrooms, sliced

1 large bunch bok choy, chopped
2 bunches green onions, chopped
Soy Dressing

Discard the seasoning packet from the noodles. Sauté the noodles and sesame seeds in the butter in a skillet until light brown. Combine the mushrooms, bok choy and onions in a salad bowl and mix well. Add the noodles, sesame seeds and Soy Dressing just before serving and toss to mix.

SOY DRESSING

1 cup salad oil
1 cup sugar

1/2 cup vinegar
3 tablespoons soy sauce

Combine the oil, sugar, vinegar and soy sauce in a bowl. Beat until well mixed and the sugar is dissolved.

▪ ▪ ▪ ▪ ▪

PEARL'S PEAS
Serves Six

1 (14 1/2-ounce) can tiny green peas
1 (14 1/2-ounce) can French green
   beans
1 (6-ounce) can sliced or button
   mushrooms

1 (2-ounce) jar chopped pimento
1 large onion, thinly sliced
1 cup apple cider vinegar
1/2 to 3/4 cup sugar
1/2 cup salad oil

Drain the peas, green beans, mushrooms and pimentos and discard the liquid. Combine the drained vegetables, onion, vinegar, sugar and oil in a bowl and mix well. Let stand, covered, in the refrigerator for 12 to 24 hours. Drain well before serving. May store in the refrigerator for 1 week.

TAHINI DRESSING

1 clove of garlic, minced
2 tablespoons lemon juice
2 tablespoons tahini
1/2 teaspoon salt
Red pepper to taste
1/4 cup water

Combine all the ingredients in a blender or a food processor container and process until well blended. This dressing is wonderful with a green salad tossed with mango slices and chopped scallions.

Tahini is a middle eastern ingredient made from ground sesame seeds. Intense in flavor, a little goes a long way. Find tahini in jars in the ethnic food section or by the peanut butter at your grocer.

BLUE RIDGE GARDEN SALAD
Serves Six

1 (15-ounce) can crowder or
  black-eyed peas
1 (15-ounce) can whole kernel corn
1 cup cooked rice
1 cup seeded and chopped plum
  tomatoes

¹/₂ cup chopped red bell pepper
¹/₂ cup sliced green onions
¹/₄ cup chopped fresh cilantro
Chile Pepper Dressing

Drain the crowder peas; rinse and drain again. Drain the corn; rinse and drain again. Combine the crowder peas, corn, rice, tomatoes, bell pepper, onions and cilantro in a bowl and mix well. Add the Chile Pepper Dressing. Toss to mix.

CHILE PEPPER DRESSING

2 dried chipotle chile peppers
¹/₄ cup fresh lime juice
2 tablespoons olive oil
1 teaspoon cumin
1 teaspoon chili powder

¹/₂ teaspoon allspice
¹/₈ teaspoon freshly ground black
  peppercorns, or to taste
¹/₈ teaspoon salt

Place the chipotle peppers in a small bowl; cover with warm water. Let stand for 30 minutes. Drain and finely chop. Combine the chopped peppers, lime juice, olive oil, cumin, chili powder, allspice, pepper and salt in a bowl and mix well.

MARINATED SLAW
Serves Twelve

1 large head cabbage
1 large onion
1 large green bell pepper
1 cup sugar
3/4 cup salad oil

1 cup vinegar
1 teaspoon dry mustard
1 teaspoon celery seeds
1 tablespoon salt

Shred the cabbage and place in a large bowl. Slice the onion and green pepper. Layer over the cabbage. Sprinkle with the sugar. Do not stir. Combine the oil, vinegar, dry mustard, celery seeds and salt in a saucepan. Bring to a boil, stirring occasionally. Pour the hot dressing over the cabbage. Chill, covered, in the refrigerator for 4 to 10 hours without stirring. Toss just before serving. Will stay crisp in the refrigerator for several days.

■ ■ ■ ■ ■

CLAREMONT SALAD
Serves Ten

2 pounds cabbage, shredded
1 large cucumber, peeled, sliced
2 carrots, peeled, shredded
1 green bell pepper, chopped
1 white or yellow onion, thinly
   sliced

1/2 cup sugar
3/4 cup vinegar
1/4 cup water
1/2 cup salad oil
4 teaspoons salt

Combine the cabbage, cucumber, carrots, green pepper and onion in a large bowl and mix well. Combine the sugar, vinegar, water, oil and salt in a bowl and stir until the sugar dissolves. Pour over the salad and mix well. Let stand, covered, at room temperature for 8 to 10 hours. Stir again. Chill, covered, until serving time. Will keep in the refrigerator for several days.

Serves Eight

¹/₂ cup olive oil	4 drops of hot pepper sauce
2 tablespoons red wine vinegar	2 heads romaine lettuce
2 tablespoons fresh lemon juice	²/₃ cup freshly grated Parmesan
1 tablespoon Worcestershire sauce	cheese
1 teaspoon Dijon mustard	Freshly grated pepper
1 teaspoon grated lemon peel	Onion Bagel Croutons
1 large clove of garlic, minced	

Combine the olive oil, vinegar, lemon juice, Worcestershire sauce, mustard, lemon peel, garlic and hot pepper sauce in a bowl, beating with a whisk. Tear the lettuce into bite-size pieces. Combine the lettuce, Parmesan cheese and pepper in a large salad bowl. Add the dressing and Onion Bagel Croutons just before serving; toss to mix.

Onion Bagel Croutons

2 small cloves of garlic, minced	1¹/₂ tablespoons olive oil
3 tablespoons butter	3 onion bagels, split

Sauté the garlic in the butter and olive oil in a skillet just until light brown. Brush the mixture onto the cut side of the bagels. Cut into croutons and place on a baking sheet. Bake at 325 degrees for 30 minutes or until brown and crisp. Cool. May store for up to 1 week in an airtight container.

Tree Trimming Dinner

CAROLINA COBB SALAD
Serves Twenty

1 head iceberg lettuce
1 head butter lettuce
1 head romaine lettuce
1 small bunch chicory
1/2 bunch watercress
2 or more tomatoes, peeled,
  chopped
6 poached chicken breast fillets,
  chopped

6 slices crisp-cooked bacon,
  crumbled
1 avocado, chopped
3 hard-cooked eggs, chopped
2 tablespoons chopped fresh chives
1/2 cup (or more) bleu or Roquefort
  cheese
1/2 pound fresh mushrooms, sliced
1 1/2 recipes Cobb Dressing

Chop all the lettuce and layer in the order listed in a large glass salad bowl. Arrange the remaining ingredients in the order listed. Add the Cobb Dressing just before serving and toss to mix.

COBB DRESSING

1 cup water
1 cup red wine vinegar
1 teaspoon sugar
Juice of 1/2 lemon
2 1/2 tablespoons salt
1 tablespoon ground pepper

1 tablespoon Worcestershire sauce
1 tablespoon Dijon mustard
1 clove of garlic, minced
1 cup olive oil
3 cups salad oil

Combine the water, vinegar, sugar, lemon juice, salt, pepper, Worcestershire sauce, Dijon mustard, garlic, olive oil and salad oil in a bowl, beating well with a whisk.

CORN BREAD SALAD
Serves Ten

1 (9-ounce) package Jiffy corn
  bread mix
1 (16-ounce) can light red kidney
  beans
32 ounces sour cream
1 cup mayonnaise
1 envelope ranch dressing mix
1 large bell pepper, chopped

1 bunch green onions, chopped
1 large tomato, chopped
1 (16-ounce) can corn, drained
1 bottle real bacon bits
2 cups shredded Colby and
  Monterey Jack cheese with
  taco seasoning

Bake the corn bread using the package directions. Cool completely; crumble. Drain the kidney beans; rinse and drain again. Combine the sour cream, mayonnaise and dressing mix in a bowl and mix well. Mix the bell pepper, onions and tomato in a bowl. Layer the crumbled corn bread, corn, beans, mixed vegetables, dressing mixture, bacon bits and cheese 1/2 at a time in a large glass salad bowl. Chill, covered, for 8 to 10 hours.

■ ■ ■ ■ ■

COUSCOUS SALAD
Serves Ten

1 cup finely chopped onion
2 tablespoons olive oil
1/2 teaspoon curry powder
1/4 teaspoon cinnamon
1/4 teaspoon cumin
Turmeric to taste
3/4 cup chicken broth
3 cups julienned carrots

1/2 cup raisins
Sherry
3 1/2 cups cooked couscous
1/2 cup pine nuts, toasted
Grated peel of 1 lemon
1/4 cup chopped fresh mint
Salt and pepper to taste

Sauté the onion in the olive oil in a large skillet over medium-low heat for 3 minutes. Add the curry powder, cinnamon, cumin and turmeric. Cook for 1 minute, stirring frequently. Add the chicken broth and carrots. Cook, covered, for 5 to 7 minutes or until the carrots are tender-crisp, stirring occasionally. Combine the raisins in a bowl with enough water and sherry to cover them. Let stand until plumped; drain. Combine the couscous, carrot mixture, raisins, pine nuts, lemon peel and mint in a large bowl and toss to mix. Add salt and pepper. Serve at room temperature.

Broccoli Salad
Serves Eight

1 cup mayonnaise
2 tablespoons white vinegar
1/4 cup sugar
Florets of 2 large bunches broccoli

1 cup golden raisins
1 small red onion, chopped
6 to 8 slices crisp-cooked bacon, crumbled

Combine the mayonnaise, vinegar and sugar in a bowl and mix well. Chop the broccoli into bite-size pieces. Combine the broccoli, raisins, onion and bacon in a bowl and toss to mix. Add the dressing, tossing to mix. Chill, covered, for several hours before serving.

■　■　■　■　■

Marinated Vegetable Salad
Serves Twelve

1 can green peas, drained
1 (14-ounce) can bean sprouts, drained
1 can chow mein vegetables, drained
1 (8-ounce) can sliced water chestnuts, drained
1 (6-ounce) can sliced mushrooms, drained

1 (16-ounce) can cut green beans, drained
1 cup chopped celery
1 small onion, finely chopped
3/4 cup apple cider vinegar
3/4 cup sugar

Combine the vegetables in a large salad bowl and mix well. Combine the vinegar and sugar in a saucepan. Bring to a boil over medium heat. Cook until the sugar dissolves, stirring constantly. Pour over the vegetables, stirring to mix. Chill, covered, for 24 hours before serving. May substitute fresh mushrooms for the canned mushrooms.

OLIVE AND ARTICHOKE SALAD
Serves Six

1 head Bibb or leaf lettuce
1 (6-ounce) jar marinated artichoke
    hearts
1/2 (10-ounce) can pitted black
    olives
2 tablespoons fresh lemon juice

1 teaspoon dried dillweed
1/4 cup olive oil
Salt and pepper to taste
1/2 cup croutons
1/4 cup Parmesan cheese

Tear the lettuce into bite-size pieces. Place in a large bowl. Drain the artichoke hearts; cut into quarters. Drain the olives; cut into halves. Add the artichokes and olives to the lettuce and toss to mix. Combine the lemon juice, dillweed, olive oil, salt and pepper in a bowl and mix well. Add to the salad; toss to mix. Add the croutons and cheese. Toss to mix.

．　．　．　．　．

CHINESE PEA SALAD
Serves Six

3/4 cup mayonnaise
1 tablespoon lemon juice
1/4 teaspoon curry powder
Garlic salt to taste
1 (16-ounce) bag frozen green peas

1 (8-ounce) can lump crab meat
1 cup chopped celery
1/2 cup cashews
1 (3-ounce) can chow mein noodles

Combine the mayonnaise, lemon juice, curry powder and garlic salt in a bowl and mix well. Place the frozen peas in a colander and hold under running cold water for several minutes to thaw; drain. Drain the crab meat. Combine the peas, crab meat and celery in a bowl and toss to mix. Add the dressing and mix well. Add the cashews and noodles just before serving. Serve on lettuce-lined salad plates. May serve the cashews and noodles on the side. May add 4 ounces cooked shrimp.

ORANGE PRALINE SALAD
Serves Eight

¹/₄ cup sugar
1 cup pecan halves
2 teaspoons sugar
¹/₂ teaspoon salt
¹/₂ teaspoon pepper
2 teaspoons balsamic vinegar

¹/₄ cup olive oil
1 large head green leaf lettuce
4 ribs celery, chopped
2 (11-ounce) cans mandarin
  oranges, drained
1 bunch green onions, chopped

Melt ¹/₄ cup sugar in a nonstick heavy skillet over low heat. Add the pecans, stirring gently until coated and golden brown. Spread on waxed paper to cool. Combine 2 teaspoons sugar, salt, pepper, vinegar and olive oil in a bowl, beating together with a whisk. Cut the lettuce into bite-size pieces. Combine the lettuce, celery, mandarin oranges and onions in a large salad bowl. Add the pecans and dressing just before serving and toss to mix. May substitute fresh orange or grapefruit sections for the mandarin oranges.

• • • • •

RASPBERRY SPINACH SALAD
Serves Six

2 tablespoons raspberry vinegar
2 tablespoons raspberry jam
¹/₃ cup corn oil
8 cups rinsed and dried fresh
  spinach

³/₄ cup chopped macadamia nuts
1 cup raspberries
3 ripe kiwifruit, sliced

Combine the vinegar and raspberry jam in a food processor container. Add the corn oil in a fine stream, processing constantly until smooth. Tear the spinach into bite-size pieces. Combine the spinach, macadamia nuts, raspberries and kiwifruit in a large salad bowl. Add the dressing just before serving and toss to mix. May substitute sliced almonds or pecans for the macadamia nuts.

Spinach Salad With Curry Dressing

Serves Eight

¹/₂ cup salad oil
¹/₂ cup white vinegar
¹/₄ cup chutney
2 teaspoons sugar
2 teaspoons dry mustard

2 teaspoons curry powder
1 (16-ounce) package spinach
2 to 3 Granny Smith apples
6 green onions, finely chopped
¹/₂ cup (or more) unsalted peanuts

Combine the oil, vinegar, chutney, sugar, dry mustard and curry powder in a blender container. Process until the chutney is puréed. Rinse the spinach; remove the stems and pat the spinach dry with paper towels. Chop the apples into bite-size pieces. Combine the spinach, apples, onions and peanuts in a bowl. Add the curry dressing and toss to mix. This is great with fish or chicken.

■ ■ ■ ■ ■

Warm Spinach And Pine Nut Salad

Serves Six

6 cups fresh spinach leaves
2 cups fresh basil leaves
¹/₂ cup olive oil
3 cloves of garlic, minced

¹/₂ cup pine nuts
4 ounces prosciutto, diced
³/₄ cup freshly grated Parmesan
  cheese

Toss the spinach and basil in a large salad bowl. Heat the olive oil in a small skillet over medium heat. Add the garlic and pine nuts. Sauté until the pine nuts are slightly brown. Stir in the prosciutto. Cook for 1 minute. Toss the spinach and basil with the warm dressing. Sprinkle with the cheese. Serve immediately. May sprinkle with freshly ground pepper.

Strawberry Vinegar

2 pints strawberries
1 quart cider vinegar
1 cup sugar

Hull the strawberries and cut into halves; place in a large stainless steel or other nonreactive saucepan. Add the vinegar. Let stand, covered, at room temperature for 1 hour. Add the sugar. Bring to a boil over medium heat, stirring occasionally. Reduce the heat. Simmer, covered, for 10 minutes. Strain, pressing the strawberries to release as much liquid as possible. Store in a covered glass container in the refrigerator. May substitute raspberries for the strawberries.

Romaine With Apple Vinaigrette
Serves Six

6 to 8 cups bite-size romaine lettuce
³/4 cup crumbled feta or bleu cheese
2 Fuji or crisp red apples, cut into chunks

¹/2 cup chopped walnuts or pecans
¹/2 to ³/4 cup Apple Vinaigrette

Combine the lettuce, feta cheese, apples and walnuts in a bowl and toss to mix. Add the Apple Vinaigrette just before serving and toss to mix.

Apple Vinaigrette

³/4 cup applesauce
¹/3 cup apple cider vinegar
1 tablespoon plus 1 teaspoon Dijon mustard

2 to 3 green onions, finely chopped
¹/4 teaspoon salt
¹/3 cup olive oil

Combine the applesauce, vinegar, mustard, onions and salt in a food processor container. Add the olive oil in a fine stream, processing constantly until smooth. Pour into a jar. Store, covered, in the refrigerator for up to 1 week. Shake or whisk just before using.

Summer Salad
Serves Variable Amount

Fresh tomatoes, peeled, sliced
Sweet onions, thinly sliced
Chopped fresh parsley, basil and
   oregano

Feta cheese, crumbled
Olive oil
Wine vinegar

Salt the tomato slices. Separate the onion slices into rings. Place a layer of tomato slices and onion rings in a large serving dish. Sprinkle with parsley, basil and oregano. Add a layer of cheese. Repeat the layers to fill the dish. Drizzle with olive oil and vinegar. This is a quick and easy salad to serve a crowd.

Tabbouleh Salad
Serves Six

2 cups hot water
1 cup uncooked bulgur wheat
1 cup chopped fresh parsley
$1/2$ cup chopped fresh mint
$1/2$ cup chopped red onion
1 cucumber, chopped

$1/3$ cup lemon juice
2 tablespoons olive oil
$1/2$ teaspoon salt
$1/2$ teaspoon pepper
2 medium tomatoes, finely chopped
Lettuce leaves

Pour the hot water over the bulgur wheat in a bowl. Let stand for 30 minutes. Drain well and press between layers of paper towels to remove any excess liquid. Combine the bulgur wheat, parsley, mint, onion and cucumber in a large bowl and mix well. Combine the lemon juice, olive oil, salt and pepper in a bowl and mix well. Add to the wheat mixture, stirring gently to mix. Chill, covered, for 8 hours. Stir in the tomatoes. Serve on lettuce-lined salad plates.

TOMATOES BABICHE
Serves Six

6 large tomatoes
Salt and pepper to taste
Powdered dill
1 (14-ounce) can artichoke hearts,
   drained

2 cups mayonnaise
1 cup sour cream
Curry powder to taste
Lemon juice to taste
Grated onion to taste

Dip the tomatoes in boiling water briefly; remove the skins. Scoop out the juice and seeds and discard. Season the tomatoes inside and out with salt, pepper and dill. Place an artichoke heart in each tomato. Place on a plate. Chill, covered, until 30 minutes before serving time. Combine the mayonnaise, sour cream, curry powder, lemon juice and grated onion in a bowl and mix well. Cover each artichoke with the sauce.

• • • • •

TOMATO PANZANELLA
Serves Four

2 large ripe tomatoes, cut into
   ³/₄-inch chunks (about 2¹/₂ cups)
¹/₄ cup chopped fresh basil
Salt and pepper to taste

Oil and Vinegar Dressing
2 cups (³/₄-inch chunks) dry
   Italian bread

Combine the tomatoes, basil, salt and pepper in a bowl and mix gently. Add the Oil and Vinegar Dressing and bread; toss to mix.

OIL AND VINEGAR DRESSING

2 tablespoons red wine or balsamic
   vinegar

1 tablespoon olive oil

Combine the vinegar and olive oil in a bowl and beat with a fork or whisk until blended.

Pasta Glossary

Fusilli: "Little Springs," spindles or spirals
Orzo: Rice-shaped or barley-shaped pasta
Acini de pepe (pastina): tiny dough, peppercorn shape
Maruzze: seashell pasta

Fresh pasta is done in the time it takes the water to return to a full boil. Dried pasta takes longer, depending on shape and size. Cook pasta al dente, completely tender, yet still firm. Test by tasting. Drain pasta in a colander, rinse quickly under cool water, and serve.

Fusilli And Feta With Fresh Sorrel
Serves Six

1 clove of garlic, minced
1/2 teaspoon salt
3/4 teaspoon pepper
3 tablespoons red wine vinegar
1/2 cup olive oil
3/4 pound fusilli noodles

3/4 pound feta cheese
1/4 cup minced red onion
1/2 cup drained chopped sun-dried tomatoes
1 cup pitted black niçoise olives
3 cups fresh sorrel leaves

Combine the garlic, salt, pepper, vinegar and olive oil in a jar with a lid. Add the top and shake vigorously to mix. Cook the noodles using the package directions for 10 minutes or just until tender; drain. Cut the feta cheese into 1/2-inch cubes. Combine the fusilli, cheese, onion, sun-dried tomatoes, olives and sorrel leaves in a bowl and toss gently to mix. Shake the dressing and add to the salad. Toss to mix. Serve at room temperature.

• • • • •

Marco Polo Salad
Serves Six

2/3 cup olive oil
1/3 cup red wine vinegar
1/2 cup chopped parsley
1 tablespoon garlic salt
1 tablespoon garlic powder
1 tablespoon ground black pepper
1/3 cup chopped walnuts or pine nuts
1 tablespoon basil

1 tablespoon oregano
1 pound bow tie pasta
1/2 pound herbed Havarti cheese
1 large red bell pepper
1 large green bell pepper
1 (7-ounce) can chopped or sliced black olives
3/4 cup grated Parmesan cheese
Salt and pepper to taste

Combine the olive oil, vinegar, parsley, garlic salt, garlic powder, pepper, walnuts, basil and oregano in a bowl and mix well. Cook the pasta using the package directions just until tender; drain. Add the dressing to the hot pasta in a large bowl. Toss to mix. Cool the pasta slightly. Cut the Havarti cheese into cubes. Cut the red and green bell peppers into strips. Add the Havarti cheese, bell peppers, olives and Parmesan cheese to the pasta, tossing to mix. Chill, covered, for up to 8 hours. Add salt and pepper just before serving.

ORZO AND ARTICHOKE SALAD
Serves Four

1¹/₂ cups orzo pasta
Salt to taste
¹/₄ cup olive oil
1 (14-ounce) can artichoke hearts,
  drained
2 ounces Parmesan cheese, freshly
  grated

2 ounces prosciutto, minced
1 to 2 tablespoons lemon juice
¹/₄ cup minced fresh parsley
4 scallions, minced
Freshy ground pepper to taste
Basil Dressing

Cook the orzo in boiling salted water using the package directions just until tender. Drain in a sieve. Rinse in cold water; drain again. Combine the orzo and ¹/₄ cup olive oil in a large bowl and toss to mix. Cut the artichoke hearts into halves. Add to the orzo; toss to mix. Add the Parmesan cheese, prosciutto, lemon juice, parsley, scallions, pepper to taste and Basil Dressing. Toss to mix. Garnish with fresh basil leaves.

BASIL DRESSING

2 tablespoons white wine vinegar
1 teaspoon Dijon mustard
Salt and pepper to taste

¹/₂ cup olive oil
2 tablespoons minced fresh basil

Combine the egg yolk, vinegar, mustard and salt and pepper in a small bowl and mix well with a whisk. Add the olive oil in a fine stream, beating well with a whisk. Add the basil and mix well.

• • • • •

SHEM CREEK PASTA SALAD
Serves Six

1 (12-ounce) package roasted garlic
  and red pepper pasta
4 to 8 ounces feta cheese, crumbled
¹/₂ Wadmalaw or other sweet onion,
  finely chopped

3 cups quartered cherry tomatoes
1 bunch fresh basil, thinly sliced
1 recipe Balsamic Vinaigrette
  (page 75)

Break the pasta into bite-size pieces. Cook the pasta using the package directions just until tender. Drain, rinse in cold water and drain. Mix the pasta, cheese, onion, tomatoes and basil in a bowl. Add the desired amount of Balsamic Vinaigrette and mix well.

PASTA BEAD SALAD
Serves Six

¹/₂ box acini di pepe pasta
2 jars marinated artichoke hearts
4 poached chicken breast fillets, chopped
¹/₂ bottle Italian dressing

Cavenders Greek seasoning to taste
Creole mustard to taste
Mayonnaise
Juice of 1 lemon

Cook the pasta using the package directions just until tender; drain. Drain the artichokes, reserving the marinade. Cut the artichokes into quarters. Combine the pasta, artichokes, artichoke marinade, chicken, Italian dressing, Greek seasoning and Creole mustard in a large bowl and toss to mix. Add enough mayonnaise to moisten the salad. Add the lemon juice and toss to mix. Chill, covered, before serving. Serve on lettuce-lined salad plates.

▪ ▪ ▪ ▪ ▪

HOLE-IN-ONE CELEBRATION

PROSCIUTTO PASTA SALAD WITH BASIL VINAIGRETTE
Serves Ten

1 cup extra-virgin olive oil
1 cup salad, canola or rice oil
1¹/₄ cups red wine vinegar
¹/₄ tablespoon chopped garlic
2 tablespoons chopped fresh basil
1 tablespoon chopped fresh parsley
¹/₄ cup sugar
8 ounces fresh mushroom caps

2 (14-ounce) cans artichoke hearts
Feta cheese
4 ounces thinly sliced prosciutto ham
1 cup cherry tomato halves
Finely chopped fresh parsley
2 cups cooked shell or tricolor rotini pasta

Combine the olive oil, salad oil, vinegar, garlic, basil, 1 tablespoon fresh parsley and sugar in a bowl and mix well. Cut the mushrooms into quarters. May cut the artichokes hearts into quarters or leave whole. Cut the feta cheese into large chunks. Coarsely chop the prosciutto ham. Combine the mushrooms, artichoke hearts, feta cheese, ham, cherry tomatoes, parsley and pasta in a large bowl. Toss gently to mix. Add the desired amount of dressing and toss to mix. Extra amounts of feta cheese and prosciutto ham make the salad tastier. May increase the amount of pasta for a large crowd without increasing the amount of the dressing.

PICCOLO PASTA
Serves Eight

8 ounces seashell pasta
1 pound pepperoni, sliced
1 pound Swiss cheese, chopped
3 tomatoes, chopped
1 teaspoon oregano
1/2 cup extra-virgin olive oil
1/4 cup cider vinegar

1 clove of garlic, minced
1 red onion, sliced
2 teaspoons salt
1/4 teaspoon pepper
1/3 cup grated Parmesan cheese
Croutons (optional)

Cook the pasta using the package directions for 8 minutes or just until tender; drain. Combine the hot pasta, pepperoni, Swiss cheese, tomatoes, oregano, olive oil, vinegar, garlic, onion, salt, pepper, Parmesan cheese and croutons if desired in a large bowl, mixing as each ingredient is added. May serve warm or chill, covered, for several hours before serving.

■ ■ ■ ■ ■

POTATO SALAD WITH BLEU CHEESE AND WALNUTS
Serves Six

2 to 3 pounds red potatoes
Salt to taste
3/4 cup crumbled bleu cheese
1/4 cup olive oil

1/4 cup fresh lemon juice
4 green onions with tops, chopped
3/4 cup chopped celery
1/2 cup coarsely chopped walnuts

Cook the potatoes in a steamer until tender; drain. Cut into small chunks. Place in a large bowl. Add salt. Combine the bleu cheese, olive oil and lemon juice in a bowl and mix well. Add to the potatoes and toss gently to mix. Add the onions, celery and walnuts and mix gently. Serve at room temperature or slightly warm. Bring to room temperature before serving if stored in the refrigerator.

HEAVENLY CRAB LOUIS
Serves Six

1/2 cup mayonnaise
1/2 cup sour cream
2 tablespoons chili sauce
2 tablespoons salad oil
1 tablespoon red wine vinegar
1 tablespoon horseradish
1 tablespoon lemon juice

1 tablespoon chopped parsley
2 teaspoons grated onion
1/2 teaspoon salt
4 drops of Tabasco sauce
1 pound lump crab meat
Lettuce or watercress

Combine the mayonnaise, sour cream, chili sauce, oil, vinegar, horseradish, lemon juice, parsley, onion, salt and Tabasco sauce in a bowl, beating well with a whisk. Chill, covered, until serving time. Place the crab meat on a bed of lettuce or watercress on a serving plate. Add the dressing. Garnish with crab claws, lemon wedges and tomatoes.

▪ ▪ ▪ ▪ ▪

SULLIVAN ISLAND SEAFOOD RICE SALAD
Serves Six

8 ounces scallops, lightly sautéed
8 ounces boiled peeled shrimp
Juice of 1 lemon
Salt to taste
1/3 cup plus 1 tablespoon red wine
    vinegar
1/2 cup saffron oil
2 teaspoons prepared mustard
Hot pepper sauce to taste

Worcestershire sauce to taste
Sugar to taste
1 (6-ounce) package yellow saffron
    rice, cooked
1 to 2 scallions, thinly sliced
1 small tomato, sliced
1 small cucumber, chopped
2 tablespoons chopped cilantro
Pepper to taste

Combine the scallops and shrimp in a bowl and toss to mix. Add the lemon juice and salt and toss gently. Chill for 2 hours. Combine the vinegar, saffron oil, mustard, hot pepper sauce, Worcestershire sauce and sugar in a bowl and mix well. Add the rice, scallions, tomato, cucumber, cilantro and pepper to the seafood and mix well. Add enough of the dressing for the desired consistency, stirring to mix well. Chill, covered, for 8 to 10 hours. May substitute honey mustard or Dijon mustard for the prepared mustard.

GRILLED TUNA PASTA SALAD
Serves Six

3/4 pound tuna steak
Juice of 1 lemon
1 tablespoon extra-virgin olive oil
1 clove of garlic, minced
1/2 teaspoon dried rosemary
3/4 pound penne or ziti pasta
1 tablespoon extra-virgin olive oil
1/4 pound green beans, trimmed
1/2 red bell pepper

1 tomato, cored, chopped
3 tablespoons chopped chives or
  scallions
Caper Dressing
Salt and pepper to taste
10 ounces fresh spinach, rinsed,
  trimmed
5 brine-cured black olives

Place the tuna steak in a large shallow bowl. Mix the juice of 1 lemon, 1 table-spoon olive oil, 1 clove of garlic and rosemary in a bowl. Pour over the tuna. Grill the tuna on a preheated grill for 5 minutes on each side or until firm and opaque throughout. Cut into bite-size pieces. Cook the pasta using the package directions just until tender. Drain; rinse and drain again. Combine the pasta and 1 tablespoon olive oil in a large bowl; toss to mix. Cut the green beans into 2-inch lengths. Blanch the beans in boiling water in a saucepan for 30 seconds; drain. Plunge into ice water; drain. Combine the tuna, pasta and green beans in a large bowl. Cut the red pepper into thin strips. Add the red pepper, tomato and chives to the pasta, tossing to mix. Add the Caper Dressing; toss to mix. Add salt and pepper to taste. Tear the spinach into bite-size pieces. Arrange the spinach in a large serving bowl or on individual serving plates. Top with the pasta salad. Garnish with black olives. The pasta salad and dressing may be refrigerated separately for several hours. Let come to room temperature and mix just before serving.

CAPER DRESSING

3 tablespoons nonfat chicken broth
3 tablespoons red wine vinegar
Juice of 1 lemon

1 teaspoon drained capers
1 clove of garlic, minced
1 teaspoon olive oil

Combine the chicken broth, vinegar, juice of 1 lemon, capers and 1 clove of garlic in a bowl and mix well. Add the olive oil gradually, beating well.

CHICKEN AND WILD RICE SALAD
Serves Six

2 to 3 cups apple juice
2 large chicken breast fillets
1 red apple with peel, chopped
1/4 cup pecans
3 cups cooked Uncle Ben's wild
   rice mix

1/2 cup finely chopped celery
1/2 teaspoon seasoned salt
1/4 teaspoon cinnamon
1/2 cup mayonnaise

Combine the apple juice and chicken in a saucepan. Simmer over low heat for 40 to 50 minutes or until the chicken is tender. Drain and chop the chicken. Combine the chicken, apple, pecans, rice and celery in a large bowl. Mix the seasoned salt, cinnamon and mayonnaise in a bowl. Add to the chicken and mix well. Chill, covered, until serving time.

· · · · ·

HOT ORIENTAL CHICKEN TOSS
Serves Six

2 cups torn romaine lettuce
2 cups torn spinach
1 (11-ounce) can mandarin oranges,
   drained
4 boneless chicken breast halves
1/3 cup flour
1/4 cup vegetable oil
3 tablespoons chopped green
   onions

2 tablespoons soy sauce
3 tablespoons water
1 tablespoon honey
1/8 teaspoon ginger
1/8 teaspoon garlic powder
1 tablespoon soy sauce
Peanuts or cashews

Combine the romaine lettuce, spinach and mandarin oranges in a large salad bowl. Cover tightly with plastic wrap. Chill for several hours. Cut the chicken into 1-inch pieces. Roll in the flour to coat. Sauté the chicken in the oil in a skillet over medium-high heat until brown on all sides. Combine the onions, 2 tablespoons soy sauce, water, honey, ginger and garlic powder in a bowl and mix well. Add to the chicken. Simmer for 5 minutes, stirring frequently. Add 1 tablespoon soy sauce to the salad; toss to mix. Pour the chicken mixture over the salad. Toss to mix. Sprinkle with peanuts.

LOWCOUNTRY LUNCHEON

VERSATILE VINEGAR

There are 4 basic kinds of vinegar: white distilled vinegar, the strongest and sharpest, is best for pickling; apple cider vinegar is preferable for cooking and pickling; wine vinegar is best for salads and sauces; and herb vinegar, often flavored with garlic, is mostly for salad dressings. Specialty vinegars, such as balsamic, rice wine, sherry, and fruit are also widely available.

JAPANESE CHICKEN SALAD
Serves Six

1¹/₂ cups mayonnaise
¹/₂ teaspoon curry powder
1 tablespoon soy sauce
4 cups chopped cooked chicken or turkey
1 (8-ounce) can sliced water chestnuts, drained

1 pound seedless grapes, cut into halves
1 cup chopped celery
1¹/₂ cups slivered almonds, toasted

Combine the mayonnaise, curry powder and soy sauce in a bowl and mix well. Combine the chicken, water chestnuts, grapes, celery and almonds in a large bowl and mix well. Add the dressing and toss to mix. Chill until serving time. Serve on lettuce-lined salad plates. Garnish with pineapple or paprika.

▪ ▪ ▪ ▪ ▪

JILLY'S LEMON CHICKEN SALAD
Serves Ten

¹/₄ cup butter
8 chicken breast fillets
¹/₂ cup white wine
Florets of 1 bunch broccoli
Salt to taste
2 large cloves of garlic, minced

1 cup mayonnaise
1 tablespoon lemon juice
¹/₂ teaspoon thyme
¹/₂ teaspoon basil
¹/₂ teaspoon oregano
Freshly ground pepper

Melt the butter in a large skillet. Add the chicken and white wine. Bring to a boil, covered, over medium heat. Reduce the heat. Simmer, covered, over low heat for 8 to 10 minutes or until the chicken is springy to the touch. Remove the chicken, reserving the pan drippings. Cool slightly. Cut into bite-size pieces. Drop the broccoli into boiling salted water in a saucepan. Cook for 30 seconds and drain. Rinse under cold water. Add the garlic to the pan drippings. Boil for 1 minute, stirring frequently. Cool the garlic-wine sauce. Combine the mayonnaise, lemon juice, thyme, basil, oregano, salt and pepper in a bowl. Add ¹/₃ cup of the garlic-wine sauce and mix well. Combine the chicken and broccoli in a large bowl. Add the mayonnaise dressing; toss to mix. Chill, covered, for 2 to 10 hours. Serve cold.

BALSAMIC VINAIGRETTE
Serves Four

¹/₄ cup balsamic vinegar
1 teaspoon (heaping) Dijon mustard

2 cloves of garlic, minced
³/₄ cup olive oil

Combine the vinegar, mustard and garlic in a blender container. Add the olive oil in a fine stream, processing constantly at high speed until smooth.

· · · · ·

FRIENDS FOR DINNER

TOMATO DRESSING
Serves Four

1 cup peeled, seeded and chopped
  tomatoes
¹/₄ cup salad oil
1¹/₂ tablespoons red wine vinegar
2 tablespoons sliced scallions
1 clove of garlic, minced

1 teaspoon thyme
¹/₄ teaspoon salt
¹/₄ teaspoon paprika
¹/₈ teaspoon sugar
Freshly ground pepper

Combine all the ingredients in a blender container. Process until puréed. This is wonderful on any salad.

Colonial Lake

Though now very contained and civilized, Colonial Lake began in a wild condition as a salt tidal estuary penetrating marshlands on the west side of colonial Charles Town. According to tradition, it was used as a small boat harbor by planters coming to town. As the city expanded, streets were run along the edges of the body of water, which became known as the Rutledge Street Pond.

It remained in a semi-natural state until the 1880s, when Mayor William Ashmead Courtenay, whose home was nearby on Lynch Street (now Ashley Avenue), had the salt pond embanked and landscaped with paved walks and benches, and renamed it Colonial Lake. It was named for the city-owned marshlands, known as the Colonial Commons, which it drained.

During the nineteenth and early twentieth centuries, the streets bordering the lake became lined with fashionable homes of prosperous Charlestonians. In this view, Rutledge Avenue is to the right and Beaufain Street is in the background. In the early twentieth century, rowboats, such as those pictured, provided access to an ice cream stand in the middle of the lake.

Bread and Breakfast

Colonial Lake, Charleston, S. C.

BREAD AND BREAKFAST

Chef Jill Hall's Romano Oregano Bread
Serves Twelve

2¹/2 tablespoons dry yeast
2 cups warm (130 degrees) water
6 cups high-gluten bread flour
1¹/2 cups grated Romano cheese

6 tablespoons sugar
2 tablespoons dried oregano
1 tablespoon salt
3 tablespoons olive oil

Proof the yeast by adding the yeast to ¹/4 cup of the warm water. Let stand until bubbly. Combine the flour, cheese, sugar, oregano and salt in a bowl, mixing well. Add the yeast and the remaining 1³/4 cups warm water and mix well. Add the olive oil and mix well. Knead on a lightly floured surface for 10 to 12 minutes or until the dough is elastic and firm but not sticky. Place the dough in a greased bowl, turning to coat the surface. Let rise, covered with a damp towel, for 1 to 1¹/2 hours or until doubled in bulk. Shape the dough into a 5x9-inch loaf or a round loaf. Place in a greased baking pan. Let rise for 1 hour or until doubled in bulk. Bake at 350 degrees for 30 to 45 minutes or until the bread tests done.

▪ ▪ ▪ ▪ ▪

*Chef Jill Hall, owner of Hall Bakery, loves everything about food.
She has worked as a sous-chef and helped other chefs open restaurants
in the Lowcountry. These experiences gave her the confidence to open
her own bakery. She and her staff bake delicious breads, pastries, cakes,
and many other mouthwatering desserts.*

DILL BREAD
Serves Twelve

3 cups self-rising flour
3 tablespoons light brown sugar
1 tablespoon dillweed

1 (12-ounce) can beer
1/4 cup melted butter

Combine the flour, brown sugar and dillweed in a bowl and mix well. Add the beer and mix well. Pour into a greased 5x9-inch loaf pan. Pour the melted butter on top. Bake at 375 degrees for 30 to 50 minutes or until the bread tests done. Do not overbake. Cool in the pan for several minutes. Remove to a wire rack.

▪ ▪ ▪ ▪ ▪

HOW TO HAVE A SHINY CRUST

To give homemade bread a shiny crust, brush the top with white or cider vinegar a few minutes before the bread is through baking.

ONION CHEESE BREAD
Serves Eight

1/2 onion, chopped
1 tablespoon canola oil
1 1/2 cups biscuit mix
1/2 cup milk
1 egg, beaten

1 teaspoon chopped parsley
8 ounces sharp American cheese, shredded
2 teaspoons melted butter

Sauté the onion in the oil in a skillet just until tender. Combine the biscuit mix, milk and egg in a bowl and mix well. Add the onion, parsley and 1/2 of the cheese; mix well. Pour into a greased 8- or 9-inch baking pan. Sprinkle the remaining cheese on top. Drizzle with the melted butter. Bake at 400 degrees for 20 minutes or until the bread tests done.

BEER BREAD

Serves Twelve

3 cups self-rising flour
2 tablespoons sugar
1/4 cup vegetable oil
1 (12-ounce) can beer

Combine the flour and sugar in a large bowl. Add the oil and beer and mix well. Pour into a greased 5x9-inch loaf pan. Bake at 350 degrees for 30 to 40 minutes or until the bread tests done. Cool in the pan for several minutes. Remove to a wire rack. Serve warm or at room temperature.

BUENO BREAD

Serves Twelve

1 cup mayonnaise
3 cups shredded Monterey Jack cheese
1/2 cup grated Parmesan cheese

1 tablespoon Worcestershire sauce
1 (4-ounce) can chopped green chiles
1 loaf sliced French bread

Combine the mayonnaise, cheeses, Worcestershire sauce and green chiles in a bowl and mix well. Spread the mixture between the slices and on top of the French bread. Wrap in foil. Bake at 350 degrees for 30 minutes. May substitute chopped cooked ham and shredded Swiss cheese for the Monterey Jack cheese and green chiles.

· · · · ·

STUFFED FRENCH BREAD

Serves Twelve

1 pound sausage
1 pound ground beef
2 medium onions, minced
1/3 cup water
1 teaspoon salt
1 egg
2 tablespoons prepared mustard

1/2 teaspoon oregano
1/2 teaspoon black pepper
2 loaves French bread
1 (4-ounce) can mushrooms, drained
Melted margarine
Garlic powder to taste

Brown the sausage and ground beef with the onions in a skillet, stirring until the sausage and ground beef are crumbly; drain. Combine the sausage mixture with the water, salt, egg, mustard, oregano and pepper in a bowl and mix well. Cut 1 slice from each end of the French bread and reserve. Cut out the center of the bread with a long serrated knife, removing the center carefully and leaving 1/4-inch shells. Crumble 1/2 of the center bread and add to the sausage mixture, mixing well. Add the mushrooms and mix well. Place the bread shells on 1 end and fill each with the sausage mixture. Replace the reserved end slices. Brush with melted margarine and sprinkle with garlic powder. Wrap in foil. Place flat on a baking sheet. Bake at 400 degrees for 10 to 15 minutes; open the foil. Cook for 5 minutes longer or until brown.

Walnut Bread
Serves Twelve

1½ cups milk
½ cup honey
1½ cups all-purpose flour
1½ cups whole wheat flour

2½ teaspoons baking powder
¾ teaspoon baking soda
¾ cup chopped walnuts or almonds

Combine the milk and honey in a bowl, stirring until well mixed. Combine the all-purpose flour, whole wheat flour, baking powder and baking soda in a large bowl and mix well. Add the milk mixture, stirring to mix well. Stir in the walnuts. Pour into a greased and floured 5x9-inch loaf pan. Bake at 275 degrees for 2 hours or until the bread tests done. Remove to a wire rack to cool. Serve, thinly sliced. Delicious served with pesto or cheese, or with Grilled Pork Tenderloin With Mustard Sauce (page 20). This bread freezes well.

· · · · ·

Orange Pecan Scones
Serves Twelve

½ cup butter, slightly softened
1¾ cups flour
⅓ cup plus 1 tablespoon sugar
1½ teaspoons baking powder
½ teaspoon baking soda
½ cup chopped pecans, toasted
Grated peel of 1 orange

½ cup orange juice
1 egg, beaten
½ cup sifted confectioners' sugar
1 tablespoon orange juice
    concentrate
1 teaspoon melted butter
12 pecan halves

Cut ½ cup butter into the flour in a bowl until crumbly. Add the sugar, baking powder and baking soda; mix well. Stir in the chopped pecans and orange peel. Mix the orange juice and egg together. Add to the batter, stirring just until mixed. Drop 12 mounds of batter onto a greased baking sheet. Bake at 375 degrees for 12 to 15 minutes or until golden brown. Cool on a wire rack. Combine the confectioners' sugar, orange juice concentrate and melted butter in a bowl and mix well. Spread a small amount of the glaze in the center of each scone; top with a pecan half.

POPPY SEED LOAVES
Serves Twenty-Four

3 cups flour
1^1/$_2$ teaspoons salt
1^1/$_2$ teaspoons baking powder
3 eggs
1^1/$_2$ cups milk
1^1/$_8$ cups vegetable oil

2^1/$_4$ cups sugar
^{1}/$_2$ to 1 tablespoon poppy seeds
1^1/$_2$ teaspoons vanilla extract
1^1/$_2$ teaspoons almond flavoring
1^1/$_2$ teaspoons butter flavoring
Orange Glaze

Combine the flour, salt and baking powder in a mixer bowl and mix well. Add the eggs, milk and oil gradually, beating well after each addition. Add the sugar, poppy seeds, vanilla, almond and butter flavoring; beat for 2 minutes. Pour into 2 greased and floured 5x9-inch loaf pans. Bake at 350 degrees for 1 hour or until the bread tests done. Cool in the pans for 5 minutes. Remove to a serving plate. Drizzle the Orange Glaze over the loaves.

ORANGE GLAZE

^{1}/$_4$ cup orange juice
^{3}/$_4$ cup confectioners' sugar
^{1}/$_2$ teaspoon butter flavoring

^{1}/$_2$ teaspoon almond flavoring
^{1}/$_2$ teaspoon vanilla extract

Combine all the ingredients in a bowl and mix well.

■ ■ ■ ■ ■

BLUEBERRY BANANA BREAD
Serves Twelve

2 cups flour
2 teaspoons baking powder
^{1}/$_2$ teaspoon salt
^{1}/$_2$ teaspoon baking soda
^{1}/$_2$ cup margarine

^{3}/$_4$ cup sugar
2 eggs
3 bananas, mashed
1 cup blueberries
^{1}/$_2$ cup chopped nuts (optional)

Sift the flour, baking powder, salt and baking soda together. Cream the margarine and sugar in a mixer bowl until light and fluffy. Beat in the eggs 1 at a time. Add the bananas and flour mixture gradually, beating well after each addition. Fold in the blueberries and nuts. Pour into a greased 5x9-inch loaf pan. Bake at 350 degrees for 1 hour or until the bread tests done. Cool in the pan for several minutes. Remove to a wire rack.

SPRING BRUNCH

Easy Banana Muffins
Makes Twelve

1 egg
1/3 cup vegetable oil
1/2 cup sugar

1 cup mashed bananas
1 1/2 cups biscuit mix
1/2 cup chopped walnuts

Combine the egg and oil in a bowl and mix well. Add the sugar and bananas and mix well. Add the biscuit mix, stirring just until combined. Stir in the walnuts. Fill greased muffin cups 2/3 full. Bake at 375 degrees for 18 to 20 minutes or until the muffins are light brown.

▪ ▪ ▪ ▪ ▪

Blueberry Oatmeal Muffins
Makes Twelve

2 cups rinsed blueberries
2 tablespoons flour
3/4 cup rolled oats
1 1/2 cups flour
3/4 cup sugar

2 teaspoons baking powder
1/2 cup butter, softened
2/3 cup milk
1 egg

Toss the blueberries and 2 tablespoons flour in a bowl until coated. Combine the oats, 1 1/2 cups flour, sugar and baking powder in a large bowl and mix well. Cut in the butter until crumbly. Add a mixture of milk and egg gradually, beating well after each addition. Fold in the blueberries. Fill greased muffin cups 2/3 full. Bake at 400 degrees for 20 to 25 minutes or until brown.

LIDIE'S ORANGE MUFFINS
Makes Twelve

2 eggs
¹/₂ cup freshly squeezed orange
   juice
¹/₄ cup sugar

2 tablespoons vegetable oil
2 cups buttermilk biscuit mix
¹/₂ cup orange marmalade

Combine the eggs, orange juice, sugar and oil in a bowl and beat well. Add the biscuit mix and beat for 30 seconds. Stir in the marmalade. Spray muffin cups lightly with nonstick baking spray. Fill the muffin cups ³/₄ full. Bake at 400 degrees for 15 minutes or until brown.

• • • • •

PUMPKIN MUFFINS
Makes Twelve

2 cups flour
1 tablespoon baking powder
¹/₂ teaspoon salt
¹/₂ teaspoon ginger
¹/₄ teaspoon nutmeg
1 teaspoon cinnamon
¹/₈ teaspoon ground cloves
²/₃ cup sugar

1 egg, beaten
1 cup sour cream
2 to 3 tablespoons sweet orange
   marmalade
¹/₃ cup vegetable oil
1 cup mashed canned or fresh
   cooked pumpkin

Sift the flour, baking powder, salt, ginger, nutmeg, cinnamon, cloves and sugar into a bowl. Mix the egg, sour cream, orange marmalade, oil and pumpkin together in a bowl. Add to the flour mixture, stirring just until mixed. The batter may be lumpy. Line muffin cups with paper or foil liners. Spray lightly with nonstick cooking spray. Fill the cups full. Bake at 400 degrees for 20 minutes or until the muffins are brown.

RASPBERRY CHEESECAKE MUFFINS
Makes Twelve

3 ounces cream cheese, softened
1 egg
¹/₃ cup sugar
¹/₂ teaspoon vanilla extract
1 cup milk
6 tablespoons butter
1 teaspoon vanilla extract

2 eggs
2 cups flour
2¹/₂ teaspoons baking powder
¹/₂ teaspoon salt
³/₄ cup sugar
1 cup fresh or frozen raspberries

Combine the cream cheese, 1 egg, ¹/₃ cup sugar and ¹/₂ teaspoon vanilla in a bowl and mix well. Combine the milk, butter and 1 teaspoon vanilla in a saucepan. Heat over low heat until the butter melts, stirring constantly. Cool just until warm to the touch. Beat in 2 eggs. Combine the flour, baking powder, salt and ³/₄ cup sugar in a bowl and mix well. Add the milk mixture, stirring just until mixed. Fold in the raspberries. Spoon into 12 greased or paper-lined muffin cups. Add 2 teaspoons of the cream cheese mixture to the top of the batter in each muffin cup, swirling slightly with a knife. Bake at 400 degrees for 20 minutes or until the tops spring back when touched.

· · · · ·

SOUR CREAM MUFFINS
Makes Twelve

¹/₂ cup melted butter
2 cups biscuit mix

1 cup sour cream

Combine the butter, biscuit mix and sour cream in a bowl and mix well. Spoon into greased muffin cups. Bake at 400 degrees for 12 to 15 minutes or until the muffins are brown.

Geeps Sulgrave Road Eggnog

Serves Twenty-Five

36 egg yolks
2 cups sugar
1 quart bourbon blend
1 pint dark rum
36 egg whites
2 quarts whipping cream,
   whipped

Beat the egg yolks in a mixer bowl until light and pale yellow. Add the sugar gradually, beating well. Add the bourbon and rum 1 drop at a time, beating constantly. This takes an eternity but it is worth the effort. Measure 2 cups of egg whites and store the remaining egg whites in the refrigerator for another use. Beat the 2 cups egg whites in a mixer bowl until stiff. Fold into the mixture. Fold in the whipped cream.

Colonial Apple Bread

Serves Twelve

3/4 cup apple cider
1 cup golden raisins
1 1/2 cups packed dark brown sugar
1/4 cup butter or margarine
1/2 teaspoon salt
3/4 teaspoon cinnamon
1/4 teaspoon cloves
1/4 teaspoon nutmeg
2 1/4 cups cake flour
1 teaspoon baking powder
1/2 teaspoon baking soda
2/3 cup chopped pecans
1 cup chopped unpeeled apple
Confectioners' sugar

Combine the apple cider, raisins, brown sugar, butter, salt and spices in a heavy saucepan. Bring to a boil over medium heat, stirring occasionally. Boil for 3 minutes, stirring frequently. Remove from the heat and cool slightly. Sift the flour, baking powder and baking soda into a large bowl. Stir the pecans and chopped apple into the cider mixture. Stir the mixture into the flour until all the ingredients are moistened. Pour into a greased bundt pan. Bake at 325 degrees for 1 hour or until the bread tests done. Cool in the pan for 10 minutes. Remove to a wire rack to cool completely. Sprinkle with the confectioners' sugar just before slicing.

· · · · ·

Most Wonderful Winter Crisp

Serves Fifteen

3 Granny Smith apples, peeled
2 cups fresh cranberries
1 (8-ounce) can juice-pack crushed
   pineapple
1/2 cup sugar
1 cup packed brown sugar
1/4 cup flour
1/2 cup butter, softened
1 cup rolled oats
1 cup chopped pecans or walnuts
Sweetened whipped cream or
   ice cream

Thinly slice the apples. Layer the apples, cranberries and pineapple with the juice in a lightly greased 9x13-inch baking dish. Sprinkle with the sugar. Combine the brown sugar and flour in a bowl and mix well. Cut in the butter until crumbly. Stir in the oats and pecans. Sprinkle over the fruit layers. Chill, covered, for 8 to 10 hours. Bring to room temperature. Bake at 375 degrees for 30 minutes or until hot and bubbly. Serve with sweetened whipped cream or ice cream.

BLUEBERRY BUCKLE
Serves Six

3/4 cup sugar
1/4 cup margarine, softened
1 egg
2 cups flour
2 teaspoons baking powder
1/2 teaspoon salt

1/2 cup milk
1 pint blueberries, rinsed, drained
1/2 cup sugar
1/3 cup flour
1/4 cup margarine, softened
1/2 teaspoon cinnamon

Cream 3/4 cup sugar and 1/4 cup margarine in a mixer bowl until light and fluffy. Beat in the egg. Mix 2 cups flour, baking powder and salt together. Add to the creamed mixture alternately with the milk, beating well after each addition. Stir in the blueberries. Pour into a greased 8- or 9-inch square baking dish. Combine the remaining sugar and flour in a bowl and mix well. Cut in 1/4 cup margarine until crumbly. Add the cinnamon and mix well. Sprinkle over the batter. Bake at 375 degrees for 25 to 30 minutes or until brown. Cool in the baking dish. Cut into servings.

· · · · ·

BAKED BLUEBERRY FRENCH TOAST
Serves Six

1 (8-ounce) loaf sourdough bread
8 ounces cream cheese, cut into
   cubes
1 pint blueberries, rinsed
1 tablespoon sugar
4 eggs

2 cups milk
1 1/2 teaspoons cinnamon
3 tablespoons confectioners' sugar,
   sifted
Blueberry syrup

Remove the crust from the bread; cut the bread into cubes. Layer 1/2 of the bread cubes and all the cream cheese cubes in a buttered 9x13-inch baking dish. Pat the blueberries dry with paper towels. Sprinkle over the cheese. Sprinkle with the sugar. Add the remaining bread cubes. Combine the eggs, milk and cinnamon in a bowl and beat well. Pour over the layers. Bake at 375 degrees for 35 to 45 minutes or until puffed and set. Sprinkle with confectioners' sugar. Serve with blueberry syrup.

Quick And Easy Blueberry Muffins
Makes Twelve

1/2 cup lowfat milk
1/4 cup vegetable oil
1 egg, slightly beaten
1 1/2 cups flour
1/2 cup sugar

2 teaspoons baking powder
1/2 teaspoon salt
1 cup well drained fresh or frozen
  blueberries

Combine the milk, oil and egg in a mixer bowl and beat well. Sift the flour, sugar, baking powder and salt together. Add to the milk mixture, stirring just until all the ingredients are moistened. Fold in the blueberries. Spoon the batter into paper-lined muffin cups, filling 1/2 full. Bake at 400 degrees for 25 minutes.

▪ ▪ ▪ ▪ ▪

Pancakes To Long For
Makes Ten

1 egg
3 tablespoons sugar
1 cup milk
1 1/4 cups sifted flour

2 1/2 teaspoons baking powder
3/4 teaspoon salt
3 tablespoons melted butter

Beat the egg in a mixer bowl. Add the sugar, milk and a mixture of the flour, baking powder and salt, beating well. Add the butter and mix well. Bake on a hot griddle, turning to brown both sides. May add chopped peaches, blueberries, strawberries or pecans.

BREAKFAST TAQUITA

Serves Eight

1 pound hot pork sausage
1 (4-ounce) can chopped green
   chiles, drained
12 eggs, lightly beaten

8 (8-inch) flour tortillas, warmed
Shredded Cheddar cheese
Picante sauce, at room temperature

Brown the sausage in a skillet, stirring until crumbly; drain. Stir in the green chiles. Add the eggs. Cook until the mixture is set. Turn the mixture. Cook until the eggs are thick but moist. Do not stir constantly. Spoon the mixture evenly down the center of each warmed tortilla. Sprinkle with cheese; add picante sauce to taste. Fold the tortilla to enclose the filling; fasten with a wooden pick. Serve immediately. May add sliced jalapeño peppers and fresh chopped cilantro.

. . . . .

CURRIED FRUIT

Serves Twelve

1 (15-ounce) can apricots, drained
1 (15-ounce) can pears, drained
1 (15-ounce) can Bing cherries,
   drained
1 (16-ounce) can peaches, drained

1 (15-ounce) can sliced pineapple,
   drained
1/2 to 1 cup butter
1/2 cup packed dark brown sugar
2 teaspoons curry powder

Arrange the fruit in a large glass casserole. Melt the butter in a skillet. Stir in the brown sugar and curry powder until well mixed. Pour over the fruit. Bake at 350 degrees for 20 to 25 minutes or until hot and bubbly. For variety combine 1 cup sherry, 1 1/2 cups white sugar and 2 tablespoons cornstarch with the butter.

CHEF ELIZABETH WARE'S GRANDMOTHER JOSIE'S GRUYÈRE GRITS SOUFFLE

Serves Six

1 quart milk
1/2 cup butter or margarine
1 (6-wedge) package Gruyère cheese
1 cup grits

1 teaspoon salt
1/8 teaspoon pepper
1/3 cup melted butter or margarine
1/2 cup grated Parmesan cheese

Bring the milk to a boil in a large saucepan. Add 1/2 cup butter and Gruyère cheese, stirring until melted. Add the grits, salt and pepper. Cook until thickened, stirring constantly. Remove from the heat. Beat for 5 minutes. Pour into a greased 2-quart soufflé dish. Pour the melted butter over the top; sprinkle with the Parmesan cheese. Bake at 375 degrees for 30 minutes.

• • • • •

*"My grandmother was an inspiration to me in my becoming a chef.
She developed many marvelous recipes and this grits soufflé is to die for.
Even people who don't ordinarily eat grits love this dish."*
Elizabeth Ware, Chef

CHEESE AND HAM SOUFFLÉ
Serves Six

1 tablespoon unsalted butter
3 tablespoons flour
1 cup milk
4 egg yolks
1 cup shredded white Cheddar
   cheese

1/2 cup finely chopped cooked
   country ham
Salt and pepper to taste
5 egg whites

Melt the butter in a large saucepan over low heat. Stir in the flour. Cook for 1 to 2 minutes, stirring constantly. Stir in the milk gradually. Bring to a simmer and cook until thickened, stirring constantly. Remove from the heat and cool. Beat in the egg yolks 1 at a time. Add the cheese, ham, salt and pepper and mix well. Beat the egg whites until soft peaks form. Add the egg whites to the egg yolk mixture 1 tablespoon at a time, beating with a whisk. Pour into a buttered and floured 2-quart soufflé dish. Bake at 400 degrees for 20 to 22 minutes or until the soufflé has risen but is still moist.

■ ■ ■ ■ ■

SEAFOOD QUICHE
Serves Six

1/2 cup mayonnaise
2 tablespoons flour
2 eggs, slightly beaten
1/2 cup milk
Salt and pepper to taste
1/4 teaspoon garlic salt
1/4 teaspoon paprika

1 (4-ounce) can sliced mushrooms,
   drained
1 cup fresh crab meat
8 ounces Swiss cheese, shredded
1/3 cup finely chopped green onions
1 unbaked (9-inch) deep-dish
   pie shell

Combine the mayonnaise and flour in a bowl and mix well. Add the eggs and milk; mix well. Stir in the salt, pepper, garlic salt, paprika and mushrooms. Add the crab meat, cheese and onions, tossing lightly to mix. Pour into the pie shell. Bake at 350 degrees for 40 to 45 minutes or until the center of the quiche is firm. May substitute shrimp or scallops for the crab meat.

POTATO AND GARLIC FRITTATA
Serves Six

4 medium red or brown potatoes
3 cloves of garlic, minced
3 tablespoons olive oil
1 small yellow onion, chopped
Salt to taste
$1/2$ teaspoon black pepper

$1/3$ cup water
4 eggs
1 tablespoon chopped fresh parsley
  or basil
$1/2$ cup freshly grated Parmesan
  cheese

Scrub the potatoes; cut into thin slices. Sauté the garlic in the olive oil in a large cast-iron or ovenproof skillet for 1 minute. Add the potatoes, onion, salt, pepper and water. Simmer for 4 to 5 minutes or until the potatoes are tender and the water is absorbed, stirring frequently. Remove from the heat. Beat the eggs and parsley together in a bowl. Place the skillet with the potatoes over medium-high heat. Cook until hot, stirring frequently. Add the eggs and stir gently to mix. Reduce the heat to low. Cook until the eggs are set, lifting gently with a spatula to let the eggs go to the bottom of the skillet. Remove from the heat. Sprinkle with the Parmesan cheese. Cook under a preheated broiler until the cheese is melted and the frittata is brown. Serve hot. May substitute 3 chopped green onions and tops for the yellow onion and use Cheddar cheese or mozzarella cheese instead of Parmesan cheese.

· · · · ·

SAUSAGE CHEESE BAKE
Serves Twelve

1 pound bulk sausage
1 large onion, finely chopped
2 cups shredded sharp Cheddar
  cheese
$1^1/2$ cups self-rising cornmeal

$3/4$ cup milk
$1/4$ cup vegetable oil
2 eggs
1 (8-ounce) can cream-style corn

Brown the sausage with the onion in a skillet, stirring until the sausage is crumbly; drain. Cool slightly. Stir in the cheese. Combine the cornmeal, milk, oil and eggs in a bowl and mix well. Stir in the corn. Layer half of the cornmeal mixture, all of the sausage and the remaining cornmeal mixture in a greased 2-quart casserole or cast-iron skillet. Bake at 425 degrees for 30 to 40 minutes or until golden brown. Let stand for 10 minutes before cutting. Serve with fruit and sour cream. May use turkey sausage for lower fat and calories.

MEETING STREET

Meeting Street was one of the original streets of the city, laid out in the 1670s as part of the "Grand Modell of Charles Town." Instructions sent by the Lords Proprietors of Carolina in 1671 called for it to be laid out 60 feet wide. The street initially had no name and later was named for the Independent Meeting House (later the Circular Congregational Church).

This early twentieth-century view looks north toward St. Michael's Church at 80 Meeting Street. The oldest church edifice in the city and one of the finest Georgian churches in the United States, St. Michael's was begun in 1752 and completed in 1771. It was designed by Samuel Cardy, an Irish builder-architect. The building stands on the site originally occupied, from circa 1682 to 1727, by the first St. Philip's Church.

In the foreground is the South Carolina Society Hall at 72 Meeting Street. The hall, built in 1804, was designed by Gabriel Manigault, the "gentleman architect," and the boldly projecting portico was added in 1825 by architect Frederick Wesner. The South Carolina Society was organized in 1737, mainly by Huguenots (French Calvinists) as a benevolent association. The scene, except for the streetcar tracks and a few other details, is unchanged today, and illustrates the ethnic, religious, and cultural diversity of historic Charleston.

Vegetables

MEETING STREET AND ST. MICHAEL'S CHURCH, CHARLESTON, S. C.

Vegetables

VICKERY'S BAR AND GRILL'S BLACK BEAN CAKES
Serves Six

1 pound black beans
1 green bell pepper, chopped
1 red bell pepper, chopped
1 medium red onion, chopped
1/8 teaspoon red pepper flakes
1/8 teaspoon chili powder

1 teaspoon cumin
1 teaspoon granulated garlic
2 cups plain bread crumbs
Olive oil
1 (16-ounce) package spinach
Balsamic vinegar

Sort and rinse the black beans. Cook the black beans using the package directions. Drain and chill, covered. Combine the black beans, green pepper, red pepper and 1/2 of the onion in a bowl and mix well. Add the red pepper flakes, chili powder, cumin, garlic and bread crumbs and mix until of a thick yet moist consistency. Shape into 3-ounce patties. Fry the patties in olive oil in a skillet over high heat, turning once. Remove to an ovenproof platter and keep warm in a 200-degree oven. Rinse and trim the spinach. Pat dry with paper towels. Add the spinach, the remaining onion and a small amount of balsamic vinegar to the pan drippings in the skillet. Cook over medium heat until the spinach wilts, stirring frequently. Remove to a serving plate. Top with the black bean cakes. Garnish with sour cream and salsa. Serve immediately.

■　■　■　■　■

Charleston's favorite watering hole since 1993, Vickery's offers
fresh seafood, Lowcountry dishes, and Caribbean dishes
in a creatively renovated old Goodyear tire store.

CAROLINA BAKED BEANS

Serves Eight

3 medium onions, chopped
2 cloves of garlic, minced
¹/₄ cup butter
¹/₂ cup packed brown sugar
¹/₄ cup cider vinegar
¹/₂ cup catsup
1 teaspoon mustard

1 (16-ounce) can butter beans,
    drained
1 (16-ounce) can kidney beans,
    drained
1 (16-ounce) can pork and beans in
    tomato sauce

Sauté the onions and garlic in the butter in a skillet until the onions are translucent. Remove from the heat. Combine the brown sugar, vinegar, catsup and mustard in a small bowl and mix well. Combine the onion mixture, brown sugar mixture, butter beans, kidney beans and pork and beans in a large bowl and mix well. Pour into a baking dish. Bake, covered, at 350 degrees for 30 minutes. Remove the cover. Bake for 15 minutes longer.

• • • • •

BEAUFAIN STREET BEANS

Serves Six

1 pound fresh young green beans
2 cups chicken broth
2 cups water
1 small onion, thinly sliced
¹/₄ cup butter

3 tablespoons freshly squeezed
    lemon juice
1 egg, beaten
1 tablespoon chopped parsley
Salt and pepper to taste

Trim the ends from the green beans and discard. Combine the green beans, chicken broth and water in a saucepan. Cook over medium heat until tender, stirring occasionally. Drain the beans. Sauté the onion in the butter in a large skillet just until soft. Add the green beans. Sauté for several minutes, stirring frequently. Add the lemon juice and egg. Cook over medium heat for 1 to 2 minutes, stirring frequently. Add the parsley, salt and pepper. Serve hot.

CONGRATULATION DINNER

COPPER HILL CHUTNEY

1 quart vinegar
3 pounds brown sugar
4 pounds ripe mangoes
1 ounce small chile peppers
2 tablespoons salt
2 pounds raisins
4 ounces fresh ginger, minced
4 ounces garlic, minced

Combine the vinegar and brown sugar in a saucepan. Boil over medium heat for 5 minutes, stirring frequently. Peel the mangoes and cut into cubes. Add to the vinegar mixture. Remove the seeds from the chile peppers and finely chop the peppers. Add the chile peppers, salt, raisins, ginger and garlic to the vinegar mixture. Simmer for 1 to 1 1/2 hours or until the fruit is glazed, stirring occasionally. Ladle into hot sterilized jars, leaving 1/4 inch of headspace; seal with 2-piece lids. Process in a boiling water bath for 10 minutes. For milder chutney use less chile peppers.

SESAME BROCCOLI
Serves Six

Florets of 1 large bunch fresh broccoli
2 tablespoons vegetable oil
2 tablespoons vinegar
2 tablespoons soy sauce
2 tablespoons sesame seeds, toasted
1 tablespoon sugar

Cook the broccoli, covered, in a small amount of water in a saucepan just until tender-crisp. Drain and arrange on a serving dish. Combine the oil, vinegar, soy sauce, toasted sesame seeds and sugar in a small saucepan and mix well. Bring to a boil over medium heat. Pour over the broccoli and serve hot.

• • • • •

LEMON-GARLIC BRUSSELS SPROUTS
Serves Four

1 pound brussels sprouts
4 cloves of garlic, minced
1 tablespoon butter
1 tablespoon olive oil
1 cup chicken broth or water
Salt and pepper to taste
1 tablespoon butter
2 tablespoons chopped parsley
1 teaspoon lemon juice

Rinse the brussels sprouts and trim off the stem ends. Cut a small X in the bottom of each sprout. Sauté the garlic in 1 tablespoon butter and olive oil in a large skillet for 2 minutes. Add the brussels sprouts, tossing gently to coat with the butter mixture. Add the chicken broth, salt and pepper. Cook, covered, over medium heat for 10 to 15 minutes or until tender. Drain. Add the remaining 1 tablespoon butter, parsley and lemon juice to the brussels sprouts in the saucepan. Heat just until the butter is melted. Pour into a serving dish.

SHOWY CAULIFLOWER
Serves Eight

1 head cauliflower
3 tablespoons Dijon
   mustard
1 cup shredded Cheddar
   cheese

Steam the cauliflower head in a steamer until tender. Drain and place on a baking sheet. Coat the surface of the cauliflower with the mustard. Sprinkle with the cheese. Broil under a preheated broiler until the cheese melts. Remove to a serving platter. Cut into slices.

JOHN'S ISLAND CARROTS
Serves Six

$^1/_2$ medium onion, chopped
1 tablespoon chopped parsley
2 tablespoons butter

10 medium carrots, peeled
1 (10-ounce) can consommé
Nutmeg to taste

Sauté the onion and parsley in the butter in a saucepan for 5 minutes. Cut the carrots into $1^1/_2$-inch pieces. Add the carrots, consommé and nutmeg to the onion. Cook, covered, over medium heat for 25 minutes, stirring occasionally. Remove the cover. Cook for 20 minutes longer or until the carrots are tender. Pour into a serving dish.

• • • • •

PORGY'S CORN PUDDING
Serves Six

6 to 8 ears fresh corn
2 to 3 egg yolks, beaten
$^1/_3$ cup sugar
$^3/_4$ cup half-and-half

3 tablespoons melted butter or
   margarine
Salt to taste
2 to 3 egg whites, stiffly beaten

Slice the corn kernels from the corncorb; scrape the corncob. Combine the corn, egg yolks, sugar, half-and-half, butter and salt in a bowl and mix well. Fold in the egg whites. Spoon into a 2-quart casserole. Place the casserole in a larger pan of boiling water. Bake at 350 degrees for 1 hour or until the center is set. If the corn browns too quickly, cover with foil.

CHEF RAMONA MEASOM'S
MUSHROOM RAGOUT
Serves Six

1 cup finely chopped shallots
Butter
1 pound mushrooms, chopped

Chicken stock
1/4 cup chopped fresh thyme

Sauté the shallots in butter in a large skillet just until translucent. Add the mushrooms. Cook, covered, over low heat until tender, stirring occasionally. Add enough chicken stock to cover the mushrooms by 1 inch. Add the thyme. Simmer over low heat for 45 minutes, stirring occasionally.

. . . . .

Chef Ramona Measom is a graduate of Johnson and Wales Culinary Institute. She has worked at Louis's Charleston Grill for Louis Osteen, one of America's premier chefs, and is currently working with Chef Osteen in his new restaurant venture. Chef Measom suggests serving the Mushroom Ragout over grits or with egg noodles.

Onion Panade
Serves Six

Salt
1½ pounds yellow onions, thinly
  sliced
4 teaspoons butter
8 ounces dry French bread, thinly
  sliced

6 ounces Parmesan cheese, grated
6 ounces Gruyère cheese, grated
Boiling salted water
Cognac
Butter

Sprinkle salt over the onion slices. Combine the onions and butter in a large skillet. Cook, covered, for 40 minutes over low heat. Remove the cover. Cook for 20 minutes or until the onions are caramelized, stirring occasionally. Spread the onions on the bread slices. Layer the bread, Parmesan cheese and Gruyère cheese ½ at a time in a 4-quart Dutch oven filling the Dutch oven only ⅔ full. Add enough boiling salted water to float the top layer. Simmer over low heat for 30 minutes. Sprinkle with cognac and dot with butter. Bake at 325 degrees for 1 hour.

. . . . .

Baked Sweet Onion
Serves Two

1 large Wadmalaw sweet onion
1 teaspoon melted butter or
  margarine

1 package instant beef bouillon
Dash of rum

Rinse and peel the onion. Cut a cone-shaped chunk out of the top of the onion, not the stem end. Fill the cavity with butter, instant bouillon and rum. Wrap in foil; place in a baking dish. Bake at 400 degrees for 35 to 45 minutes or until the onion is soft. May also place in a covered glass baking dish and microwave on High for 5 minutes or until the onion begins to turn transparent. Remove the cover. Bake at 400 degrees for 10 minutes.

Squash Parmesan
Serves Six

2 pounds yellow squash and
   zucchini, sliced
Salt to taste
2 (16-ounce) cans stewed tomatoes
1 teaspoon garlic powder
2 teaspoons flour
1 teaspoon salt

2 teaspoons sugar
1 teaspoon paprika
$1/8$ teaspoon pepper
$1/8$ teaspoon basil
8 ounces mozzarella cheese,
   shredded
$1/2$ cup grated Parmesan cheese

Combine the yellow squash and zucchini with a small amount of salted water in a saucepan. Cook over medium heat for 10 minutes or until tender-crisp, stirring occasionally; drain. Combine the stewed tomatoes, garlic powder, flour, 1 teaspoon salt, sugar, paprika, pepper and basil in a saucepan and mix well. Simmer over low heat until thickened, stirring constantly. Alternate layers of the squash, mozzarella cheese, tomatoes and Parmesan cheese in a greased 2-quart casserole until all ingredients are used. Bake, covered, at 350 degrees for 1 hour.

. . . . .

Wadmalaw Squash Casserole
Serves Six

8 yellow squash, sliced
4 zucchini, sliced
1 medium onion, chopped
Salt to taste

1 cup sour cream
3 or 4 dashes Worcestershire sauce
Pepper to taste
$3/4$ cup shredded Cheddar cheese

Combine the squash, zucchini and onion with a small amount of salted water in a saucepan. Cook over medium heat for 10 minutes or until tender-crisp; drain. Combine the squash mixture, sour cream, Worcestershire sauce, salt and pepper in a bowl and mix well. Pour into a greased casserole. Sprinkle with the cheese. Bake at 350 degrees for 30 minutes.

ROSEMARY BAKED POTATOES

Scrub baking potatoes and cut into halves lengthwise. Spray a baking sheet with nonstick cooking spray. Arrange rosemary sprigs on the baking sheet. Place the potatoes cut-side down on the rosemary. Bake at 400 degrees for 45 minutes or until the potatoes are tender. Transfer the potatoes to a serving dish; discard the rosemary.

PLANTATION SQUASH
Serves Six

6 medium yellow squash
1 (10-ounce) package chopped
  spinach
3 ounces cream cheese, softened
1 egg, beaten
2 tablespoons melted butter
1/2 to 1 teaspoon pepper

3/4 teaspoon sugar
1/4 teaspoon seasoned salt
1/4 teaspoon onion salt
1/2 cup butter cracker crumbs
Paprika
4 slices crisp-cooked bacon,
  crumbled

Place the whole squash in a small amount of water in a saucepan. Bring to a boil and reduce heat. Simmer, covered, for 8 to 10 minutes or until tender-crisp; drain and cool. Trim off the stems; cut into halves lengthwise. Scoop out the pulp and drain. Cook the spinach using the package directions and omitting the salt; drain. Mash the squash pulp in a bowl. Add the spinach and cream cheese and mix well. Add the egg, butter, pepper, sugar, seasoned salt and onion salt and mix well. Spoon into the squash shells. Sprinkle with the cracker crumbs, paprika and crumbled bacon. Place on a lightly greased baking sheet. Bake, covered with foil, at 325 degrees for 30 minutes. May freeze before baking.

• • • • •

CAPERS ISLAND ROASTED POTATOES
Serves Four

12 red potatoes
2 tablespoons olive oil
1 1/2 teaspoons Mixed-Up Salt

1 teaspoon pepper
Rosemary, chives and parsley
  to taste

Scrub the potatoes; cut into quarters. Steam or boil the potatoes in water in a saucepan for 5 minutes. Place in a sealable plastic bag. Add the olive oil, salt, pepper and herbs. Seal the bag and shake to mix. Place the potatoes on a greased baking pan. Bake at 450 degrees for 45 minutes. May turn off oven and hold for several minutes or until serving time. The potatoes will be crispy on the outside and tender on the inside.

CRAB-STUFFED POTATOES
Serves Four

4 large baking potatoes
1/2 cup butter, softened
1/2 cup cream
1 teaspoon salt
1/8 teaspoon cayenne
1/2 small onion, finely grated

1 cup shredded sharp Cheddar cheese
1 teaspoon paprika
1 (6-ounce) can crab meat, picked, drained

Bake the potatoes at 400 degrees for 1 hour. Increase the oven temperature to 450 degrees. Cut the potatoes into halves lengthwise. Scoop out the potato pulp, reserving the shells. Mash the potato pulp in a bowl until all the lumps are mashed. Add the butter, cream, salt, cayenne, onion, cheese and 1/2 teaspoon paprika and mix well. Fold in the crab meat. Spoon into the reserved potato shells; sprinkle with the remaining 1/2 teaspoon paprika. Place on a baking sheet. Bake at 450 degrees for 15 minutes or until heated through and slightly brown.

. . . . .

LEMON BASIL ROASTED POTATOES
Serves Four

2 1/2 pounds red or Yukon gold potatoes
1/4 cup olive oil
2 tablespoons fresh lemon juice
1 teaspoon salt

1/4 teaspoon paprika
1/2 teaspoon freshly ground pepper
1 tablespoon chopped fresh basil
1 tablespoon chopped fresh chives

Scrub the potatoes; pat dry with paper towels. Combine the olive oil, lemon juice, salt, paprika and pepper in a roasting pan and stir to mix. Add the potatoes; turn with a spoon to coat with the oil mixture. Roast the potatoes at 425 degrees for 45 minutes or until golden brown and tender, turning every 15 minutes. Transfer to a serving dish. Sprinkle with basil and chives.

LATKES (POTATO PANCAKES)
Serves Six

3 large round potatoes, coarsely
  chopped
1 onion, coarsely chopped
1 egg
1/2 teaspoon salt

Pepper to taste
1 teaspoon baking powder
1/4 to 1/2 cup flour
Vegetable oil for frying

Combine the potatoes and onion in a food processor. Process until finely
chopped and well mixed. Combine the potato mixture, egg, salt, pepper and a
mixture of baking powder and flour in a bowl and mix well. Heat about 1/2 inch
of oil in a skillet. Drop the potato mixture by spoonfuls into the hot oil. Fry until
golden brown; drain on paper towels. Place on an ovenproof serving platter and
keep warm in a 200-degree oven. Serve with applesauce.

• • • • •

PECAN TOPPING

1 cup pecans
1/3 cup self-rising flour
Salt to taste
Cinnamon to taste
1/2 cup sugar or brown sugar

Combine pecans, flour, salt,
cinnamon and sugar in a bowl
and mix well.

SWEET POTATO CASSEROLE
Serves Six

3 cups mashed cooked fresh
  sweet potatoes
1 cup sugar
2 eggs
1/2 cup milk
1/2 teaspoon salt

1 teaspoon vanilla extract
Cinnamon to taste
1/2 cup butter
Pecan Topping (at left)
1/4 cup melted butter

Combine the sweet potatoes, sugar, eggs, milk, salt, vanilla and cinnamon in a
bowl and mix well. Spoon into a shallow baking dish. Dot with 1/2 cup butter,
pressing into the sweet potatoes. Sprinkle with the Pecan Topping. Drizzle with
the melted butter. Bake at 350 degrees for 45 minutes. May substitute 1/4
teaspoon orange flavoring for the cinnamon.

Snow Peas And Carrots
Serves Six

3 large carrots, peeled
Water
1/4 cup minced shallots
2 tablespoons butter

1 pound fresh snow peas
2 tablespoons dry sherry
Salt and freshly ground pepper
   to taste

Cut the carrots into slices diagonally. Bring water to a boil in a saucepan over medium heat. Add the carrots. Simmer for 2 minutes. Drain and rinse with cold water. Sauté the shallots in the butter in a large skillet for 1 minute. Add the carrots and snow peas, turning to coat with the butter. Add the sherry. Cook for 3 minutes, stirring frequently. Season with salt and pepper. Serve immediately.

• • • • •

Spinach Pasta Pie
Serves Six

1 (10-ounce) package frozen
   chopped spinach, thawed
6 ounces vermicelli
2 tablespoons butter, softened
1/3 cup grated Parmesan cheese
2 eggs, beaten
1/3 cup milk

4 ounces shredded mozzarella
   cheese
3 eggs, beaten
1/4 teaspoon pepper
1/8 teaspoon nutmeg
6 (3-inch) strips pimento

Drain the spinach, pressing out the moisture. Cook the pasta using the package directions for 8 minutes; drain. Combine the hot pasta, butter and Parmesan cheese in a bowl and mix well. Add 2 beaten eggs and mix well. Spoon the mixture into a greased 9-inch pie plate, shaping into a pie shell. Cover with foil. Bake at 350 degrees for 10 minutes. Remove the foil and cool. Combine the spinach, milk, mozzarella cheese, 3 eggs, pepper and nutmeg in a bowl and mix well. Spoon the mixture into the pasta pie shell. Cover with foil. Bake at 350 degrees for 45 minutes. Remove the cover. Bake for 10 minutes longer. Arrange the pimento strips on the top, radiating out from the center. Let stand for 10 minutes before slicing.

Spinach Pie

Serves Twelve

1 (10-ounce) package frozen
   chopped spinach, thawed
1/2 cup melted margarine
1 (9-ounce) package Jiffy
   corn bread mix
4 eggs
6 ounces cottage cheese
2 large onions, chopped

Drain the spinach, pressing
out the moisture. Combine the
margarine, corn bread mix and
eggs in a bowl and mix well.
Add the spinach, cottage
cheese and onions and mix
well. Pour into 2 greased pie
plates. Bake at 400 degrees for
25 to 30 minutes or until the
centers are set.

Torta Di Spinacci

Serves Six

1 (10-ounce) package frozen
   chopped spinach, thawed
1 (10-ounce) package frozen
   artichoke hearts
1/2 medium sweet onion, chopped
4 ounces (5 slices) Genoa salami,
   chopped

1 clove of garlic, minced
1/4 cup olive oil
1/2 teaspoon nutmeg
Salt to taste
2 tablespoons olive oil
1/2 cup grated Parmesan cheese
1/2 cup shredded mozzarella cheese

Drain the spinach, pressing out the moisture. Thaw the artichokes partially.
Sauté the onion, salami and garlic in 1/4 cup olive oil in a skillet over medium
heat for 3 minutes. Add the spinach, nutmeg and salt and mix well. Sauté for 3
minutes. Spoon into a greased 8-inch deep-dish pie plate. Let cool for 5 minutes.
Stir-fry the artichokes in the remaining 2 tablespoons olive oil in a skillet over
medium heat until light brown. Add the cheese to the spinach mixture and stir
gently to mix. Arrange the artichokes on top of the spinach. Cover with waxed
paper. Microwave on High for 2 minutes. Serve hot. May bake, covered with foil,
at 325 degrees for 15 minutes.

Spinach And Artichoke Casserole

Serves Eight

2 (10-ounce) packages frozen
   chopped spinach, thawed
1 cup chopped onions
1/2 cup chopped celery
1/2 cup butter

1 cup sour cream
1 cup grated Parmesan cheese
Salt and pepper to taste
1 (15-ounce) can artichoke hearts

Cook the spinach using the package directions. Drain the spinach, pressing out
the moisture. Sauté the onions and celery in the butter in a skillet. Combine the
spinach, onion mixture, sour cream, 1/2 cup of the Parmesan cheese, salt and
pepper in a bowl and mix well. Drain the artichokes; rinse and drain again. Chop
the artichokes coarsely. Add to the spinach mixture and mix well. Spoon into a
buttered 2-quart casserole. Top with the remaining 1/2 cup Parmesan cheese.
Bake at 350 degrees for 30 minutes or until bubbly.

STIR-FRY VEGETABLES
Serves Six

2 tablespoons canola oil
1 tablespoon minced gingerroot
2 onions, chopped
Florets of 1 pound fresh broccoli
8 ounces snow peas
8 green onions, sliced

4 ribs celery, diagonally sliced
8 ounces spinach, chopped
³/₄ cup water
1 tablespoon instant chicken
  bouillon

Heat the oil in a wok over high heat. Add the gingerroot, chopped onions and broccoli. Stir-fry for 1 minute. Add the snow peas, green onions, celery and spinach. Stir-fry for 1 minute. Add a mixture of the water and instant chicken bouillon. Bring to a boil, stirring constantly. Cook, covered, for 2 to 3 minutes or just until the vegetables are tender-crisp.

· · · · ·

TIAN OF SUMMER VEGETABLES
Serves Twelve

¹/₄ cup olive oil
2 summer squash
2 zucchini
1 medium eggplant
1 or 2 Vidalia or other sweet onions
5 medium ripe tomatoes
2 or 3 different colored Holland
  peppers

1 teaspoon each chopped fresh
  thyme, oregano, rosemary and
  basil
Salt and freshly ground black
  pepper to taste
2 tablespoons freshly grated
  Parmesan cheese

Coat a 10-inch round baking dish with 1 tablespoon of the oil. Rinse the vegetables and trim off the ends. Cut the vegetables into very thin round slices. Arrange the vegetables slightly overlapping from the outside edge of the baking dish, standing the slices on their edges and interchanging colors to form an appealing pattern. Pack the slices tightly so they will stay in place during baking. Sprinkle with the chopped herbs, salt and pepper. Drizzle with the remaining 3 tablespoons olive oil; cover with foil. Bake at 375 degrees for 40 to 45 minutes or just until the squash is tender. Sprinkle with the Parmesan cheese. Garnish with whole fresh herbs. Serve hot.

Chef Elizabeth Ware's
Tian De Courgettes Et De Tomatoes
(Tomato And Zucchini Casserole)
Serves Four

1 large sweet onion, thinly sliced
5 tablespoons extra-virgin olive oil
2 to 3 cloves of garlic, minced
5 or 6 firm ripe tomatoes
5 small zucchini, thinly sliced

Salt and freshly ground pepper
Chopped fresh thyme and basil
  leaves
Freshly grated Parmesan or Gruyère
  cheese

Sauté the onion in 2 tablespoons olive oil in a heavy 9-inch ovenproof skillet until soft. Add the garlic. Sauté for 1 minute. Remove from the heat. Remove the cores of the tomatoes; cut into slices. Layer the tomatoes and zucchini on top of the onions in the skillet in long overlapping rows, alternating tomatoes and zucchini. Sprinkle with salt, pepper, thyme and basil. Drizzle with the remaining 3 tablespoons olive oil. Bake at 450 degrees for 30 minutes. Sprinkle with the Parmesan cheese. Bake for 5 minutes longer or until the cheese is melted. May serve hot or at room temperature.

. . . . .

This recipe is my own version of a dish I tried while living with a French family one summer after high school. We travelled to the south of France to the hills above Cannes called Grosse. This simple rustic peasant dish is a great accompaniment to beef, pork or lamb dishes. My French Mama grew up in Grosse and made this for me.

TOMATO PIE

Serves Six

1 unbaked (9-inch) deep-
   dish pie shell
2 to 3 medium tomatoes
1 Vidalia onion, thinly sliced
1/2 teaspoon salt
1/4 teaspoon pepper
1/2 teaspoon dried basil
1/4 teaspoon chopped green
   onions
1/1 cup mayonnaise
1 cup shredded Cheddar
   cheese

Prick the pie shell with a fork in 4 or 5 places. Bake the pie shell at 400 degrees for 5 minutes. Peel the tomatoes and remove the core. Cut into slices. Layer the tomato slices in the pie shell. Top with the onion slices. Sprinkle with salt, pepper, basil and green onions. Mix the mayonnaise and cheese in a bowl. Spread over the layers, sealing to the edge. Bake at 400 degrees for 30 minutes.

TOMATOES STUFFED WITH ZUCCHINI AND YELLOW SQUASH

Serves Six

6 medium tomatoes
Salt to taste
1 pound zucchini
1 pound yellow squash
1/2 cup chopped yellow onion
1 clove of garlic, minced
2 tablespoons unsalted butter
2 to 3 tablespoons heavy cream
3/4 cup shredded Swiss cheese
Pepper to taste
Olive oil
Grated Parmesan cheese

Cut off the top 1/3 of the tomatoes. Scoop out the insides; sprinkle with salt. Drain on paper towels for 30 minutes. Cut the zucchini and yellow squash into 2-inch pieces; cut into 1/4-inch julienne. Place in a colander and sprinkle with salt. Let drain for 30 minutes. Wrap in a towel and squeeze out the remaining moisture. Sauté the onion and garlic in the butter in a skillet until soft. Add the zucchini and yellow squash. Sauté over high heat for 2 minutes or just until tender-crisp. Add the cream. Cook over high heat for 3 minutes or until the cream is reduced, stirring frequently. Remove from the heat. Stir in the Swiss cheese and salt and pepper to taste. Rub olive oil on the drained tomatoes. Stuff with the squash mixture. Place on a baking sheet. Sprinkle with Parmesan cheese. Bake at 350 degrees for 20 to 25 minutes.

• • • • •

CREOLE ZUCCHINI

Serves Eight

5 to 6 zucchini
Salt
1 large onion, chopped
1 (16-ounce) can tomatoes
1/2 teaspoon chopped basil
Creole seasoned salt to taste

Cut the zucchini into slices. Combine with a small amount of salted water in a saucepan. Cook over medium heat just until tender, stirring occasionally; drain. Spray a large heavy skillet with nonstick cooking spray. Sauté the onion in the skillet until soft. Add the undrained tomatoes, basil, seasoned salt and zucchini. Simmer for 15 minutes or until most of the liquid is evaporated, stirring frequently.

WEST POINT RICE MILL

Rice was the primary crop of the South Carolina Lowcountry from the early Colonial period into the early twentieth century. Its adjunct, rice milling, was one of Charleston's main industries during the antebellum period when the city ranked third in industrial importance in the South. The West Point Rice Mill was built in 1860 by a group of local businessmen. The picture depicts the mill in the early twentieth century flanked by two buildings more utilitarian in design.

Named for its location on the West Point of the Charleston peninsula overlooking the Ashley River, the mill operated until 1927. This view shows a three-masted sailing vessel, possibly carrying rice, anchored near the mill wharf. In 1937, the mill building was rehabilitated by the City of Charleston and the Works Progress Administration, and made the terminus of a trans-oceanic seaplane service. During World War II, it was the office building and recreation center for the Minecraft Base, U.S. Navy. Afterwards, the area in front of the mill was redeveloped as the City Marina.

The mill building was rehabilitated again in 1966 for the headquarters of the Charleston Trident Chamber of Commerce. After being heavily damaged by Hurricane Hugo in 1989, it was rehabilitated again and now houses offices and a popular restaurant at 17 Lockwood Drive.

Rice and Pasta

WEST POINT RICE MILLS. CHARLESTON. S. C.

Ashley River — Loaded with b

RICE AND PASTA

GULLAH RICE
Serves Six

2 cups uncooked rice
1 medium bell pepper, chopped
1 medium onion, chopped

1 (10-ounce) can beef consommé
1 (10-ounce) can beef broth
1/2 cup melted butter

Combine the rice, bell pepper, onion, consommé, broth and butter in a bowl and mix well. Pour into a greased 2-quart glass baking dish. Bake, covered, at 350 degrees for 1 hour.

• • • • •

HOPPIN' JOHN WITH A KICK
Serves Twenty

1 package cow peas or field peas
1 package neck bones or ham
  chunks
1 pound hot or medium sausage
1 pound mild sausage

1 large onion, chopped
2 cups uncooked converted rice
Hot pepper sauce to taste
Salt and pepper to taste

Prepare peas the night before using. Cook the peas according to package directions, adding neckbones or ham chunks. Let cool. Remove meat from neckbones and return to the peas. Chill overnight. Brown all the sausage with the onion in a skillet, stirring until the sausage is crumbly; drain. Cook the rice using the package directions. Combine the peas mixture, sausage, rice, hot pepper sauce, salt and pepper in a large saucepan. Simmer over low heat for 1 to 1 1/2 hours, stirring occasionally.

HOT AND SPICY RICE
Serves Eight

12 ounces sliced bacon
2 cups uncooked long grain rice
1 (32-ounce) can stewed tomatoes,
   mashed
2 medium onions, chopped

1/4 teaspoon salt
Pepper to taste
1 small jar picante sauce
1/4 teaspoon Tabasco sauce, or
   to taste

Cook the bacon in a skillet until brown and crisp. Remove the bacon with a slotted spoon and drain, reserving 2 tablespoons bacon drippings in the skillet. Add the rice, tomatoes, onions, salt, pepper, picante sauce, Tabasco sauce and bacon to the reserved bacon drippings and mix well. Simmer over low heat for 10 minutes. Pour into a greased 9x13-inch baking dish. Cover tightly with foil. Bake at 350 degrees for 1 hour, fluffing with a fork after 30 minutes.

■ ■ ■ ■ ■

LOWCOUNTRY RICE PILAF
Serves Six

2 yellow onions, chopped
1 clove of garlic, minced
1 tablespoon butter
5 ounces kielbasa sausage, chopped

2 cups water
1 cup rice
1 (16-ounce) can corn, drained

Sauté the onions and garlic in the butter in a large saucepan. Add the sausage. Cook over medium heat until brown, stirring frequently. Add the water and rice. Bring to a simmer. Cook, covered, over low heat for 30 minutes. Stir in the corn. Let steep, covered, for 10 minutes before serving.

MARKET STREET RICE
Serves Six

2 cups uncooked rice
1/2 cup chopped celery
1/2 cup chopped bell pepper
1 bunch green onions with tops,
    chopped

1/2 cup butter
1 (4-ounce) jar diced pimentos
1 (4-ounce) can sliced black olives

Cook the rice using the package directions. Sauté the celery, bell pepper and onions in the butter in a large skillet until almost soft. Add the pimentos, olives and rice. Heat to serving temperature, stirring frequently. Serve immediately.

• • • • •

MIDDLETON WILD RICE CASSEROLE
Serves Four

1 cup uncooked wild rice
3 green onions with tops, sliced
1 (4-ounce) package slivered
    almonds

3 tablespoons butter or margarine
3 cups hot chicken broth

Sauté the rice, onions and almonds in the butter in a large skillet until the onions are soft and the almonds are beginning to brown. Pour into a greased casserole. Pour the chicken broth over the rice mixture. Bake, covered, at 325 degrees for 1 1/2 hours. Stir and serve. This is great with turkey, chicken, beef and pork dishes.

This is always served at our Thanksgiving dinner.
It goes great with turkey, chicken, beef and pork dishes.

BEACH HOUSE DINNER

BEAUREGARD STREET RED RICE

Serves Eight

4 to 6 slices bacon
1 medium onion, finely chopped
1 (14-ounce) can whole tomatoes
Salt and pepper to taste
2 tablespoons hot sauce

2 tablespoons (or more) catsup
1 or 2 large smoked hot or mild
   sausages
3 to 4 cups uncooked rice
$1/2$ tomato can water

Cut the bacon into 2-inch pieces. Fry the bacon with the onion in a large skillet until brown. Add the tomatoes and liquid, chopping the tomatoes into bite-size pieces. Add salt, pepper, hot sauce and catsup. Chop the sausage into bite-size pieces. Add the sausage and rice to the mixture. Bring to a boil over medium heat. Reduce the heat. Simmer, covered, over low heat for 30 to 45 minutes or until the rice is soft, stirring every 10 to 15 minutes and adding the water $1/8$ cup at a time if the rice is sticking. If there is too much liquid remove the cover.

．　．　．　．　．

RED BEAN PESTO WITH PASTA

Serves Six

3 to 4 cups loosely packed sweet
   basil
4 medium cloves of garlic, peeled
$1/4$ cup olive oil
1 (15-ounce) can red kidney beans

$1/2$ cup freshly grated Parmesan
   cheese
Salt and pepper to taste
1 pound pasta, cooked

Rinse the basil; pat dry with paper towels. Combine the basil, garlic and 3 tablespoons of the olive oil in a food processor container. Process until finely chopped. Drain the beans; rinse and drain again. Add the beans, Parmesan cheese and remaining 1 tablespoon olive oil to the food processor container. Process until coarsely chopped, adding more olive oil if necessary to make a paste-like texture. Add salt and pepper to taste. Serve over hot pasta. May store for 4 to 6 months in the freezer but add the salt and pepper just before using. Red Bean Pesto is also delicious on boiled new potatoes, or as a spread on bread or crackers.

Broad Street Pasta
Serves Ten

1 pound macaroni noodles
3 cups lowfat cottage cheese
3 cups shredded sharp Cheddar
   cheese
8 ounces lowfat sour cream

1 egg, lightly beaten
1/2 teaspoon dry mustard
1/4 teaspoon white pepper
2 drops of Worcestershire sauce
Paprika to taste

Cook the macaroni using the package directions; drain. Rinse and drain again.
Combine the cottage cheese, Cheddar cheese, sour cream, egg, dry mustard,
pepper and Worcestershire sauce in a bowl and mix well. Stir in the macaroni.
Spoon into a greased 2-quart baking dish. Sprinkle with paprika. Bake at 350
degrees for 45 minutes.

．　．　．　．　．

Fresh Tomato And Green Pepper Pasta
Serves Six

6 tomatoes, thinly sliced
6 green bell peppers, thinly sliced
1 clove of garlic, minced
2 tablespoons chopped fresh basil
1 cup olive oil

Salt and pepper to taste
16 ounces uncooked spaghetti
1 cup shredded mozzarella cheese
1 cup grated Parmesan cheese

Combine the tomatoes, green peppers, garlic, basil, olive oil, salt and pepper in a
bowl and mix gently. Chill, covered, for 8 to 10 hours. Cook the spaghetti just
until tender using the package directions; drain. Spoon the spaghetti onto heated
serving plates. Add the tomato marinade. Sprinkle with equal amounts of
mozzarella and Parmesan cheese.

Basic Vegetarian Pasta Sauce
Serves Twelve

1 (28-ounce) can whole tomatoes
1 (15-ounce) can tomato sauce
1 (12-ounce) can tomato paste
2 cloves of garlic, minced
1 large onion, coarsely chopped
2 tablespoons olive oil or water
2 large carrots, sliced
1 rib celery, finely chopped

1/4 small green bell pepper, finely chopped
2 bay leaves
1 teaspoon dried basil
1 teaspoon dried parsley
1 teaspoon black pepper
1/2 teaspoon salt
1/2 teaspoon dried oregano

Combine the tomatoes and liquid, tomato sauce and paste in a slow cooker, breaking up the tomatoes into bite-size pieces. Sauté the garlic and onion in the olive oil in a large skillet just until soft. Add the carrots, celery and green pepper. Cook just until heated through, stirring frequently. Add to the tomatoes. Add the remaining ingredients, mixing well. Cook on Low for 6 to 8 hours, stirring every 2 to 3 hours if possible. May be simmered in a large stockpot over low heat for 1 hour or longer, stirring frequently to prevent sticking. Remove the bay leaves and discard before serving.

Pasta Sauce Variations

Add chopped cooked chicken, cooked ground beef, whole cooked chicken breasts, whole cooked pork chops, whole or chopped mushrooms, sliced zucchini or yellow squash, peeled sliced or cubed eggplant, or chopped red or yellow bell peppers to the tomato mixture while cooking. Add cooked shrimp just before serving. The sauce freezes well. Use for baked pastas, lasagna and omelettes, or on top of grilled breads or opened mussels.

Oriental Linguini
Serves Six

1 pound linguini
1/4 cup peanut oil
1 1/2 cups mayonnaise
5 teaspoons soy sauce
5 teaspoons Dijon mustard

Hot chili oil to taste
1 bunch green onions, trimmed
Asparagus tips
Snow peas or broccoli florets

Cook the linguini using the package directions; drain. Combine the linguini and peanut oil in a large bowl and toss to mix. Let cool to room temperature. Whisk the mayonnaise, soy sauce, mustard and hot chili oil in a bowl. Add to the linguini. Cut the green onions into diagonal slices. Add to the linguini, tossing to mix. Pour into a serving bowl. Garnish with asparagus tips and snow peas.

• • • • •

Stono River Sesame Noodles
Serves Six

1 pound thin spaghetti
2 tablespoons sesame oil
1/4 cup peanut butter or sesame
  paste
1/4 cup soy sauce
2 tablespoons wine vinegar

1 tablespoon fresh ginger, minced
1/4 teaspoon crushed red pepper
1 red bell pepper, diced
4 scallions, chopped
Toasted sesame seeds or chopped
  peanuts

Cook the spaghetti using the package directions; drain. Combine the spaghetti and sesame oil in a bowl and toss to mix. Combine the peanut butter, soy sauce, vinegar, ginger, red pepper, bell pepper and scallions in a bowl and mix well. Add to the spaghetti, tossing to mix. Chill, covered, until serving time. Sprinkle with sesame seeds or peanuts just before serving. May be served cold or at room temperature. This is a great cookout or picnic dish.

PENNE PASTA WITH FRESH ASPARAGUS AND CARAMELIZED ONIONS

Serves Four

1 pound fresh asparagus
1/4 cup olive oil
1 large clove of garlic, thinly sliced
1 tablespoon kosher salt

1/2 to 3/4 pound uncooked penne
   pasta
Caramelized Onions
Parmesan cheese

Trim the asparagus; cut into 2-inch diagonal slices. Combine the asparagus, olive oil and garlic in a baking dish. Sprinkle with the salt. Roast on the top rack of a 500-degree oven for 10 to 15 minutes, stirring the asparagus once or twice. Cook the pasta using the package directions; drain. Combine the roasted asparagus mixture, pasta, Caramelized Onions and Parmesan cheese in a bowl and toss to mix. Pour into a serving dish.

CARAMELIZED ONIONS

2 yellow onions, thinly sliced
3 to 4 tablespoons olive oil
2 to 3 tablespoons butter or
   margarine

1 teaspoon brown sugar

Combine the onions, olive oil, butter and brown sugar in a large skillet, mixing well. Cook over medium-low heat for 20 to 30 minutes or until the onions are soft and golden brown, stirring frequently.

THYME PARSLEY PESTO AND PASTA
Serves Four

1/2 cup fresh thyme
1 cup fresh parsley
4 cloves of garlic, peeled
1 cup grated Parmesan cheese

1 cup walnuts
1/2 cup olive oil
4 cups hot cooked pasta

Process the thyme in a food processor until very finely chopped. Add the parsley, garlic, Parmesan cheese and walnuts. Process until finely chopped and well mixed. Add the oil slowly, pulsing the processor until the pesto is paste-like. Serve over hot pasta. May also serve with boiled new potatoes, or on bread or crackers. May store in the refrigerator for up to 1 week.

▪ ▪ ▪ ▪ ▪

BASIL PESTO AND PASTA
Serves Four

3/4 cup pine nuts or chopped toasted
  walnuts
3 cups loosely packed fresh basil
  leaves
1 cup grated Parmesan cheese

4 to 5 cloves of garlic, peeled
Salt and pepper to taste
1/2 to 3/4 cup olive oil
4 cups hot cooked pasta

Combine the pine nuts, basil, Parmesan cheese, garlic, salt and pepper in a food processor container. Process until mixed to a coarse texture. Add the olive oil slowly, processing constantly at high speed until the pesto is paste-like. Add to the hot pasta and toss to mix. May freeze in an ice cube tray, tightly covered with foil, for later use. May also spread the pesto on sliced French bread and toast in the oven.

ROTINI WITH SPINACH
Serves Eight

1 package tricolor rotini pasta
2 cloves of garlic, minced
$1/2$ cup chopped green onions
$1/4$ cup olive oil
3 cups chopped tomatoes

1 (16-ounce) package fresh spinach, trimmed
8 ounces feta cheese, crumbled
$1/2$ cup pine nuts, toasted
Salt and pepper to taste

Cook the pasta using the package directions; drain. Sauté the garlic and onions in the olive oil in a large saucepan just until soft. Add the tomatoes and spinach. Cook for 2 minutes, stirring frequently. Pour over the pasta and toss to mix. Add the cheese, pine nuts, salt and pepper and toss to mix. Substitute drained and chopped canned tomatoes when fresh tomatoes are out of season.

. . . . .

GRANDMA'S SPAGHETTI
Serves Eight

$1^1/2$ pounds ground beef
1 slice whole wheat bread, cubed
1 onion, chopped
1 bell pepper, chopped
2 cloves of garlic, minced
Salt to taste
$1/2$ to $3/4$ teaspoon basil
1 teaspoon oregano

$1/2$ cup chopped fresh parsley
1 (28-ounce) can whole tomatoes, chopped
1 (6-ounce) can tomato paste
1 (6-ounce) can tomato sauce
$1/2$ pound uncooked spaghetti
Grated Parmesan cheese

Brown the ground beef with the cubed bread in a large skillet, stirring until crumbly; drain, reserving the pan drippings. Sauté the onion, bell pepper and garlic in the pan drippings in a small skillet. Stir in the salt, basil, oregano and parsley. Cook the tomatoes in a saucepan over low heat for 45 minutes, stirring occasionally. Stir in the tomato paste and tomato sauce. Add the tomato mixture and the onion mixture to the ground beef. Cook, covered, over low heat for 1 hour, stirring occasionally. Cook the spaghetti using the package directions; drain. Pour into a serving bowl. Add the ground beef sauce and sprinkle with Parmesan cheese.

VEGETARIAN DINNER

Spinach Angel Hair And Red Pepper Cream Sauce

Serves Eight

1 pound spinach angel hair pasta
1 pound chicken or veal, chopped
Olive oil
1 ounce fresh dill
1 (8-ounce) jar oil-pack sun-dried
   tomatoes

6 ounces pine nuts
Red Pepper Cream Sauce
Parmesan cheese

Cook the pasta just until tender using the package directions; drain. Sauté the chicken or veal in olive oil in a skillet. Add the dill, sun-dried tomatoes and pine nuts. Sauté until heated through. Add the Red Pepper Cream Sauce. Heat to serving temperature. Toss with the hot pasta. Serve on warm plates. Sprinkle with Parmesan cheese. May substitute chicken or veal that has been marinated in Italian dressing and grilled for the sautéed chicken or veal.

Red Pepper Cream Sauce

6 red peppers, or 3 or 4 (7-ounce)
   jars roasted red peppers
1 to 2 cups white wine

32 ounces heavy cream
Salt and pepper to taste

Char the red peppers on a grill until blackened on all sides. Seal in a paper bag for several minutes. Peel the charred skin off under cold water. Chop the peppers. Combine the peppers and the wine in a large saucepan. Cook over low heat until almost all the wine is evaporated, stirring frequently. Add the cream. Cook until reduced by 1/4. Purée in a food processor until smooth. Season with salt and pepper.

INDIGO WHARF LASAGNA
Serves Eight

1 pound Italian sausage
1 clove of garlic, minced
1 tablespoon dried basil
1½ teaspoons salt
1 (16-ounce) can diced tomatoes
2 (6-ounce) cans tomato paste
1 cup water
6 to 8 lasagna noodles

Salt to taste
2 eggs
3 cups ricotta cheese
¼ cup Romano cheese
1 teaspoon salt
1 pound thinly sliced or grated
   mozzarella cheese

Remove the sausage from the casing. Brown the sausage in a large skillet, stirring until crumbly; drain. Add the garlic, basil, 1½ teaspoons salt, tomatoes, tomato paste and water. Simmer, covered, over low heat for 15 minutes, stirring occasionally. Cook the noodles in salted water using the package directions. Drain; rinse and drain again. Beat the eggs in a bowl. Add the ricotta cheese, Romano cheese and 1 teaspoon salt, mixing well. Layer the noodles, ricotta cheese mixture, mozzarella cheese and meat sauce ½ at a time in a baking dish sprayed with nonstick cooking spray. Bake at 375 degrees for 30 minutes or until hot and bubbly. Let stand for 10 minutes before cutting into servings. May be refrigerated before baking and baked for 45 minutes. May use part-skim ricotta cheese.

HERB'S CHICKEN PASTA
Serves Eight

1 pound fettuccini or linguini
1¹/₂ cups sliced fresh mushrooms
¹/₂ cup chopped onion
1 clove of garlic, minced
1 teaspoon olive oil
6 chicken breast fillets, cut into
   strips

¹/₂ teaspoon salt
¹/₂ teaspoon dried basil
Freshly ground pepper
2 cups chopped fresh tomatoes
Grated Parmesan cheese

Cook the fettuccini using the package directions; drain. Sauté the mushrooms, onion and garlic in the olive oil in a large skillet for 2 minutes. Add the chicken, salt, basil and pepper. Cook for 5 minutes or until the chicken is cooked through. Add the tomatoes. Cook for 2 to 4 minutes. Combine with the pasta in a bowl and toss to mix. Sprinkle with Parmesan cheese. Serve with crusty bread and a fresh green salad. Artichoke hearts may be added to the chicken just before mixing with the pasta and heated just to serving temperature.

▪ ▪ ▪ ▪ ▪

CRAB SCHALLAU OVER LINGUINI
Serves Six

1 pound linguini
1 medium onion, chopped
1 medium green bell pepper,
   chopped
2 cloves of garlic, minced
¹/₂ cup olive oil

1 teaspoon hot sauce
1 tablespoon Worcestershire sauce
1 (14-ounce) can tomatoes, chopped
1 (6-ounce) can tomato paste
2 cups crab meat

Cook the linguini using the package directions; drain. Sauté the onion, green pepper and garlic in the olive oil in a large skillet. Add the hot sauce, Worcestershire sauce, tomatoes and tomato paste. Simmer over low heat for 10 to 15 minutes. Stir in the crab meat. Heat to serving temperature. Serve over the hot linguini.

THE EXCHANGE BUILDING

Maritime trade was important to the Charleston economy from the early colonial period. Its significance is illustrated by The Old Exchange Building and Custom House, circa 1767-1771, at the foot of Broad Street. Designed by William Rigby Naylor, an Irish architect, it was the most impressive public building in British America.

A public meeting on December 3, 1773, to protest the Tea Tax, resulted in the establishment of a Patriot government for South Carolina. Patriot authorities stored seized British tea in the Exchange and hid gunpowder in the basement during the British occupation in 1780-1782. The British used the basement as a dungeon for political and military prisoners.

When Charleston was incorporated in 1783, the building became the City Hall. President George Washington was welcomed to Charleston here in May 1791, and a magnificent concert and ball were held in his honor. The building was the U.S. Post Office from 1818 to 1894, except for the Civil War period when it was the Confederate Post Office.

The Rebecca Motte Chapter of the Daughters of the American Revolution acquired the property in 1917. The Exchange Building was rehabilitated in 1979-1983 as a project for the American Revolution Bicentennial.

Meats

C. T. 10—Exchange Building,
Charleston, S. C.
"America's Most Historic City"

MEATS

Mr. Burbage's Roast Beef

Serves Variable Amount

1 beef roast	1 cup hot water
Lemon juice	1 medium onion, chopped
Soy sauce	1 (10-ounce) can beef broth or
Garlic salt	consommé
Coarsely ground black pepper	1 broth can water

Pat the roast dry with paper towels. Place on a rack in a roasting pan. Baste with lemon juice and soy sauce. Sprinkle with garlic salt and black pepper. Pour the hot water into the roasting pan to prevent the pan drippings from burning. Bake at 350 degrees for 18 minutes per pound for rare, 22 minutes per pound for medium-rare and 28 minutes per pound for well done. Add the onion to the pan drippings after 30 minutes of baking to make gravy. Add the broth and water to the gravy during the last 30 minutes of baking.

■ ■ ■ ■ ■

Burbage's, Charleston's oldest corner grocery store, has been open for 50 years. It has been at the current location, 157 Broad Street, for 36 years. Owner Robert A. Burbage opened the grocery store to provide the neighborhood with quality groceries, fresh meats, and service. Today, his oldest son, Alvin Burbage, is the owner. Burbage's still provides downtown Charleston with friendly service, top cuts of beef, fresh chickens, homemade sausage, homemade soups and salads, and a fine selection of gourmet cheeses.

BALSAMIC BUTTER SAUCE

Make an elegant sauce after sautéing or roasting meat or poultry by stirring about ¼ cup balsamic or wine vinegar into the browned drippings in the pan. Cook for 1 to 2 minutes; add 1 to 2 tablespoons cold butter, swirling the pan until the butter melts. Season and serve with the meat.

BRUCE'S BEEF TENDERLOIN
Serves Variable Amount

1 whole beef tenderloin
1 pound fresh mushrooms, thinly sliced
2 red bell peppers, sliced lengthwise
2 yellow bell peppers, sliced lengthwise

½ cup Worcestershire sauce
1 cup soy sauce
Cavender's Greek seasoning

Place the beef on a large piece of heavy-duty foil. Arrange the mushrooms and bell pepper strips over the beef. Pour the Worcestershire sauce and soy sauce over the beef; sprinkle liberally with Cavender's Greek seasoning. Wrap the beef in the foil, double folding the edges to seal. Cook on a grill over high heat for 40 minutes for medium-rare to rare doneness. This is a great meal for a large group. Serve with grilled or twice-baked potatoes and other vegetables.

· · · · ·

FLANK STEAK TERIYAKI
Serves Variable Amount

1 tablespoon vegetable oil
½ cup soy sauce
¼ cup sugar
2 tablespoons sherry
1 teaspoon ground ginger

1 clove of garlic, minced
½ teaspoon MSG
1 flank steak
4 to 6 pineapple slices

Combine the oil, soy sauce, sugar, sherry, ginger, garlic and MSG in a bowl and mix well. Place the flank steak in a shallow dish. Pour the marinade over the steak. Marinate, covered, in the refrigerator for 1 to 1½ hours. Drain the steak, reserving the marinade. May make pinwheels from the steak before cooking by rolling ¾-inch strips of steak and securing with a wooden pick. Place the steak on a rack in a broiler pan. Broil 4 to 5 inches from the heat source for 7 minutes, basting once with the reserved marinade. Turn the steak. Broil for 5 to 7 minutes longer, basting once with the marinade. Add the pineapple to the broiling rack during the last 3 to 4 minutes of cooking, basting once with the marinade. Serve the steak and pineapple over a bed of wild rice garnished with cherry tomatoes and parsley.

Beef Tenderloin With Bleu Cheese Sauce
Serves Four

2 tablespoons butter, softened
2 pounds beef tenderloin,
  membrane removed
Salt to taste
1/4 cup sliced scallions

2 tablespoons marjoram
2 tablespoons soy sauce
1 teaspoon Dijon mustard
3/4 cup sherry
Bleu Cheese Sauce

Spread the butter over the beef; sprinkle lightly with salt. Place in a roasting pan. Bake at 400 degrees for 20 minutes. Combine the scallions, marjoram, soy sauce, mustard and sherry in a saucepan. Bring to a boil over medium heat, stirring occasionally. Pour over the beef. Bake for 15 to 25 minutes or to desired doneness; 20 minutes is equivalent to medium doneness. Serve with the Bleu Cheese Sauce.

Bleu Cheese Sauce

3/4 cup madeira
2 tablespoons minced shallots
1 cup heavy cream
1/2 cup brown beef stock
6 ounces bleu cheese, crumbled,
  softened

1/2 cup butter, softened
Salt and cayenne pepper to taste
Paprika to taste

Combine the madeira and shallots in a saucepan. Cook over medium heat until reduced to approximately 1/4 cup, stirring frequently. Stir in the cream and stock. Cook over medium heat until reduced to 1 cup, stirring frequently. Combine the cheese and butter in a bowl and mix well. Whisk the cheese mixture into the sauce. Reduce the heat. Simmer for 3 minutes, stirring constantly. Strain the sauce. Stir in salt, cayenne pepper and paprika.

Mom's Marinade

1 cup olive oil
1 tablespoon tarragon
  vinegar
1 tablespoon brown sugar
1 package dry Italian
  dressing mix
1 cup soy sauce

Combine all the ingredients
in a bowl and mix well. Pour
the marinade over the meat
in a shallow bowl. Marinate,
covered, in the refrigerator for
up to 48 hours before cooking.
This is excellent for beef
tenderloin.

Blackened New York Strip
Serves Four

1 (3/4-pound) New York strip steak,
  2 1/2 to 3 inches thick
1/2 teaspoon dried thyme
1/2 teaspoon dried oregano
1/4 teaspoon salt
1/2 teaspoon freshly ground black
  pepper
1/2 teaspoon ground red pepper
1 tablespoon olive oil

Trim the excess fat from the steak and discard. Combine the thyme, oregano,
salt, black pepper and red pepper in a bowl. Crush with the back of a spoon
and mix well. Pat the mixture into the steak, spreading evenly over the top and
bottom. Heat the oil in a heavy ovenproof skillet over medium-high heat. Add the
steak. Cook for 3 minutes on each side. Place the skillet in a 450-degree oven.
Bake for 20 to 25 minutes or to desired doneness. Remove from the oven. Cover
with foil and let stand for 10 minutes. Cut into thin slices. May add 1/2 teaspoon
rosemary to the seasoning.

• • • • •

Italian Meat Loaf
Serves Six

2 pounds ground chuck beef
1 package hot Italian sausage,
  casing removed
3 eggs
3 slices bread, torn into bite-size
  pieces
Garlic to taste
Coarse black pepper to taste
1/4 pound bleu cheese, crumbled
1 (16-ounce) can Italian tomatoes,
  mashed

Combine all the ingredients in a bowl and mix well. Shape into a loaf; place in a
greased baking dish. Bake at 350 degrees for 1 hour, draining several times. Let
stand for 15 minutes before slicing.

BEEF ACAPULCO
Serves Four

1 pound ground beef or bulk
  sausage
1 large onion, chopped
1 clove (or more) of garlic, minced
1 tablespoon (or more) olive oil
1 (14-ounce) can stewed tomatoes
1 envelope taco seasoning mix
1 cup water

1 teaspoon ground cumin
Flour tortillas
8 ounces Monterey Jack cheese,
  grated
$1/3$ cup (or more) chopped jalapeño
  peppers
$3/4$ cup sour cream
Black olive halves

Brown the ground beef with the onion and garlic in the olive oil in a skillet, stirring until the ground beef is crumbly; drain. Add the tomatoes, taco seasoning mix, water and cumin. Simmer, covered, over low heat for 20 minutes, stirring occasionally. Spoon a layer of sauce into a 9x13-inch baking dish. Layer the tortillas, cheese, jalapeño peppers, sour cream and remaining sauce $1/2$ at a time in the prepared dish, ending with the sauce. Cover with olives. Bake, covered, at 350 degrees for 20 to 30 minutes or until bubbly. May substitute tomato sauce or thick salsa for the stewed tomatoes. Add additional tomatoes if the layers are too dry. May be frozen before or after baking.

. . . . .

BABOUTI
Serves Four

$1^{1/4}$ pounds ground beef or lamb
2 medium onions, chopped
1 (15-ounce) can peeled tomatoes
1 green bell pepper, chopped
1 cucumber, chopped
1 apple, chopped

1 cup raisins
1 cup slivered almonds
1 teaspoon apricot jam
Curry powder to taste
Salt and pepper to taste
1 banana, sliced

Brown the ground beef with the onions in a skillet, stirring until the ground beef is crumbly; drain. Add the tomatoes, green pepper, cucumber, apple, raisins and almonds and mix well. Stir in the apricot jam, curry powder, salt and pepper. Add the banana. Simmer over low heat for 45 minutes, stirring occasionally. Serve over rice with Syrian bread, shredded coconut, chutney, raisins, peanuts and chopped cucumbers.

LOWCOUNTRY VEAL AND SHRIMP
Serves Six

6 to 8 slices veal
2 eggs, beaten
1½ cups Italian-seasoned bread
  crumbs
¼ cup grated Parmesan cheese

3 tablespoons olive oil
1 (14-ounce) can whole artichokes
½ pound peeled and deveined
  shrimp, rinsed
3 tablespoons butter

Dip the veal slices in the beaten eggs. Combine the bread crumbs and Parmesan cheese in a bowl and mix well. Dip the veal in the bread crumbs to coat. Brown the veal on both sides in the oil in a nonstick skillet. Remove to a serving platter. Keep warm in a 250-degree oven. Pour the artichokes and liquid into a skillet. Cook over low heat for 5 minutes or until the liquid is reduced by half, stirring constantly. Cool the artichokes; cut into quarters. Sauté the shrimp in the butter in a skillet until pink. Add the artichokes and remaining liquid. Simmer for several minutes to blend the flavors. Pour over the veal and serve.

· · · · ·

VEAL PARMESAN WITH SPAGHETTI
Serves Six

6 thin slices veal
6 tablespoons olive oil
½ cup chopped onion
¼ cup chopped green bell pepper
⅓ cup white wine
1 pound tomatoes, chopped
2 (8-ounce) cans tomato sauce

1 (6-ounce) can tomato paste
1 clove of garlic, minced
1 tablespoon chopped parsley
1 teaspoon chopped oregano
½ pound long spaghetti noodles
6 ounces sliced mozzarella cheese

Pound the veal with a meat hammer until very thin. Brown the veal in the oil in a skillet. Remove the veal to a platter. Sauté the onion and green pepper in the pan drippings until the onion is clear. Add the white wine, tomatoes, tomato sauce, tomato paste, garlic, parsley and oregano; mix well. Add the veal. Simmer over low heat for 30 minutes, stirring occasionally. Cook the spaghetti using the package directions. Drain and pour into a serving bowl. Add ½ of the sauce and mix well. Add the cheese to the remaining sauce and veal in the skillet. Simmer, covered, for 5 minutes. Spoon over the spaghetti and serve immediately.

EMMA LAW'S CRANBERRY SAUCE
Serves Eight

2 cups sugar
6 tablespoons frozen orange
   juice concentrate
1 cup dry white wine
1 pound fresh cranberries

Combine the sugar, orange
juice concentrate and wine in a
4- to 5-quart saucepan. Cook
over low heat until the sugar
dissolves, stirring constantly.
Add the cranberries. Bring to
a boil. Cook over medium
heat for 7 to 10 minutes or
until the cranberries pop open,
stirring frequently. Pour into
a refrigerator container. Chill,
covered, until serving time.

BRAISED LAMB SHANKS
Serves Three

3 lamb or veal shanks
1 1/2 tablespoons olive oil
1 red onion, finely chopped
2 large carrots, sliced
3 cloves of garlic, minced
1 cup dry red wine
1 cup beef broth
1 1/2 tablespoons tomato paste
1/2 cup chopped seeded and peeled
   tomato
1/4 teaspoon thyme
1 small bay leaf
Salt and freshly ground pepper to
   taste
Chopped fresh parsley

Brown the lamb shanks on all sides in the oil in a large skillet. Remove to a
platter. Sauté the onion and carrots for 10 minutes in the pan drippings. Add the
garlic. Sauté for 1 minute. Add the red wine, beef broth, tomato paste, tomato,
thyme, bay leaf, salt and pepper; mix well. Add the lamb shanks. Bring to a boil
over medium heat. Reduce the heat. Simmer, covered, for 2 hours. Stir the
mixture. Simmer for 30 minutes longer. Remove the bay leaf and discard. Pour
into a serving dish. Garnish with the parsley. May use fresh or canned tomato.

▪ ▪ ▪ ▪ ▪

LEG OF LAMB
Serves Ten

1/2 cup margarine, softened
1 teaspoon sugar
1 teaspoon Worcestershire sauce
1/4 cup flour
1/4 cup apple cider vinegar
1 tablespoon salt
Pepper to taste
2 cloves of garlic, minced
1 teaspoon dried tarragon
1 (6 pounds or more) leg of lamb

Combine the margarine, sugar, Worcestershire sauce, flour, vinegar, salt, pepper,
garlic and tarragon in a bowl and mix well to form a thick paste. Place the lamb
fat side up in a roasting pan. Spread the margarine paste over the surface of the
lamb. Bake the lamb at 400 degrees for 10 minutes. Reduce the temperature to
350 degrees. Bake for 10 minutes. Reduce the temperature to 300 degrees. Bake
for 1 hour per pound or until done to taste, basting frequently with the pan
drippings. If the drippings become too thick, add equal amounts of beef broth
and water.

Chef Paul Theos' Souvlaki
Serves Four

2 pounds pork tenderloin
Fresh onions, green bell peppers
   and mushrooms
1/2 cup olive oil
1/4 cup lemon juice

1/4 cup red wine vinegar
2 cloves of garlic, minced
1 teaspoon dried oregano
Salt and pepper to taste

Remove the silver skin and fat from the tenderloin and discard. Cut the tenderloin into serving sizes. Cut the vegetables into chunks. Thread about 8 ounces of tenderloin onto each of 4 skewers, alternating with the vegetables. Combine the olive oil, lemon juice, vinegar, garlic, oregano, salt and pepper in a bowl and mix well. Place the shish kabobs in a shallow dish. Pour the marinade over the shish kabobs. Marinate, covered, in the refrigerator for 2 hours. Cook on a hot grill until cooked through, turning to brown both sides.

▪ ▪ ▪ ▪ ▪

*Paul Theos' Greek heritage marries well with his love for cooking.
Niko's Cafe, his first restaurant venture, specializes in old family recipes
and is a favorite with locals and tourists alike.*

Apricot-Marinated Pork Kabobs
Serves Six

2 pounds pork tenderloin
2 (8-ounce) cans pineapple chunks, drained
4 cloves of garlic, minced
4 shallots, finely chopped
1/2 cup olive oil
2 teaspoons cilantro

1/2 teaspoon salt
1/2 teaspoon black pepper
1/2 teaspoon red pepper flakes
1/3 cup soy sauce
1/4 cup red wine vinegar
1 (10-ounce) jar apricot preserves

Cut the pork tenderloin into cubes. Thread the pork onto skewers, alternating with the pineapple chunks. Place in a shallow dish. Combine the garlic, shallots, olive oil, cilantro, salt, pepper, red pepper flakes, soy sauce, vinegar and apricot preserves in a bowl and mix well. Pour over the kabobs. Marinate, covered, in the refrigerator for at least 1 hour. Cook on a hot grill for 3 minutes on each side or until cooked through.

· · · · ·

Albemarle Point Marinade For Ham
Serves Variable Amount

1/2 cup ginger ale
1/2 cup orange juice
1/4 cup packed light brown sugar
1/8 teaspoon ground ginger
1/2 teaspoon ground cloves

1 teaspoon dry mustard
1 1/2 teaspoons wine vinegar
1 or 2 (3/8-inch) slices
  center-cut ham

Combine the ginger ale, orange juice, brown sugar, ginger, cloves, dry mustard and vinegar in a bowl and mix well. Place the ham in a nonmetallic container. Pour the marinade over the ham. Marinate, covered, in the refrigerator for 24 hours. Cook on a hot grill for 10 minutes on each side or until done to taste. May substitute 1/2 teaspoon grated fresh ginger for the ground ginger.

HOLIDAY PORK ROAST
Serves Twelve

1 head of garlic
1 (about 5 pounds) boneless pork
   loin roast
Freshly ground black pepper
1/4 to 1/2 cup melted butter or
   margarine

1 cup dry white wine
3 Granny Smith apples
1/2 cup packed brown sugar
1/2 to 3/4 cup half-and-half or heavy
   cream

Separate the garlic into cloves, cutting into halves if large. Cut slits into the pork roast and insert the garlic. Place in a sealable plastic bag. Chill in the refrigerator for 4 to 6 hours. Remove from the bag and place in a roasting pan. Cover with black pepper, melted butter and wine. Bake, covered, at 350 degrees for 2 hours. Cut the apples into chunks. Place in a plastic bag with the brown sugar. Seal the bag and shake to coat the apples. Place the apples around the roast in the pan. Bake for 15 minutes longer. Remove the roast to a serving platter. Arrange the apples around the roast. Pour the half-and-half into the pan drippings. Cook over medium heat on top of the stove until thickened, stirring frequently. Serve with the roast.

. . . . .

CRUSTY PORK TENDERLOIN
Serves Twelve

1 tablespoon paprika
2 1/2 teaspoons salt
1 teaspoon onion powder
1 teaspoon ground red pepper
3/4 teaspoon white pepper

3/4 teaspoon black pepper
1/2 teaspoon dried thyme
1/2 teaspoon dried oregano
4 pork tenderloins

Combine the paprika, salt, onion powder, red, white and black pepper, thyme and oregano in a bowl and mix well. Coat the pork with the spices. Let stand, covered, for 1 hour in the refrigerator. Cook over very hot coals, under a broiler or in a 450-degree oven for 10 to 15 minutes or until cooked through, depending on the thickness of the tenderloin. Do not overcook. Cut into very thin slices. Serve hot or cold.

AUTUMN DINNER

CHEF JAMES BURNS' JALAPENO MARINATED PORK TENDERLOIN WITH SWEET PEACH CHUTNEY

Serves Four

2 (12- to 14-ounce) pork tenderloins
1 jalapeño pepper, thinly sliced
1 clove of garlic, minced
1 teaspoon cracked black pepper

1 teaspoon kosher salt
2 to 3 tablespoons olive oil
Sweet Peach Chutney

Trim the silver skin from the pork tenderloins and discard. Combine the jalapeño pepper, garlic, black pepper, salt and olive oil in a bowl and mix well. Rub over the pork tenderloin and place in a shallow dish. Chill, covered, for 6 hours to overnight. Cook on a hot grill until cooked through. Serve with Sweet Peach Chutney.

SWEET PEACH CHUTNEY

12 to 16 fresh peaches
4 cups white vinegar
3/4 cup sugar
3/4 cup packed light brown sugar

1/2 teaspoon mustard seeds
1/2 teaspoon celery seeds
1/2 teaspoon crushed red pepper
1 teaspoon salt

Peel the peaches and cut into slices, discarding the pits. Combine the vinegar, sugar, brown sugar, mustard seeds, celery seeds, red pepper and salt in a large saucepan. Bring to a boil over medium heat. Cook for 5 minutes, stirring occasionally. Add the peaches. Cook until small bubbles start to surface, stirring occasionally. Pour into a bowl. Let cool. Chill, covered, in the refrigerator. May store for 3 to 4 weeks in the refrigerator.

J. Bistro opened with rave reviews in November of 1995. Chef/Owner James Burns pulled from experiences in world-class kitchens and created what is considered by many to be the best restaurant in Charleston. You can catch James on the Discovery Channel in Great Chefs of the South and America series. He can also be found at his new venture, Bistro To Go, right next to his restaurant, J. Bistro, located in Mt. Pleasant.

GRAND MARNIER CRANBERRY SAUCE

Serves Six

1 (12-ounce) package
  cranberries
1 cup sugar
1 teaspoon grated orange
  peel
2 tablespoons Grand
  Marnier liqueur

Rinse and drain the
cranberries. Combine the
cranberries, sugar and orange
peel in a saucepan. Do not
add water. Cook over low
heat until the mixture comes
to a boil, stirring occasionally.
Simmer over low heat for 8
minutes, stirring frequently.
Remove from the heat. Stir in
the Grand Marnier. Cover and
let stand for 20 minutes. Pour
into a bowl. Store, covered, in
the refrigerator.

SPECIAL STUFFED CROWN ROAST OF PORK

Serves Twelve

1 (12- to 16-rib) crown roast of pork
1 tablespoon olive oil
Salt and pepper to taste
1 pound sweet Italian sausage,
  casing removed
1/2 cup water
2 tablespoons olive oil
4 cups finely chopped onions
2 cups finely chopped carrots
2 cups finely chopped celery
2 cloves of garlic, minced
7 medium potatoes, peeled, diced
1/3 cup chopped parsley
1 teaspoon fennel seeds, crushed
1/4 teaspoon pepper

Brush the roast with 1 tablespoon olive oil. Sprinkle with salt and pepper to taste
and wrap the bones with foil to prevent burning. Place the roast in a shallow
roasting pan. Roast at 475 degrees for 15 minutes. Reduce the oven temperature
to 325 degrees. Roast for 1 to 1 1/2 hours. Cook the sausage with the water in
a skillet, breaking up the sausage with a spoon. Cook until the water has
evaporated and the sausage is brown, stirring frequently. Remove the sausage
with a slotted spoon and drain on paper towels. Add 2 tablespoons oil to the
pan drippings. Sauté the onions, carrots, celery and garlic in the pan drippings
over medium heat for 15 to 20 minutes or until the carrots are tender. Boil the
potatoes in water to cover in a saucepan for 10 minutes or until tender, stirring
occasionally; drain. Combine the sausage, sautéed vegetables, potatoes, parsley,
fennel seeds and 1/4 teaspoon pepper in a bowl and mix well. Fill the center of
the roast with the stuffing, mounding slightly. Place extra stuffing in a glass
baking dish. Cover and bake with the roast. Roast at 325 degrees for 45 to 60
minutes longer or until a meat thermometer inserted in the center of the roast
registers 170 degrees. Remove the foil. Place the roast on a serving platter. Serve
with the stuffing.

SAVORY BEEF STEW
Serves Six

2 pounds (1-inch) stew beef cubes
2 tablespoons canola oil
1 (28-ounce) can whole tomatoes,
  cut into fourths
1/2 cup coarsely chopped onion
2 teaspoons Worcestershire sauce
1 clove of garlic, minced
1 bay leaf
1 teaspoon sugar

1/4 teaspoon ground thyme
Coarsely ground black pepper to
  taste
4 medium potatoes, peeled, cubed
4 medium carrots, peeled, cubed
2 ribs celery, sliced
3/4 cup hot water
Salt to taste

Brown the beef cubes in the oil in a Dutch oven, stirring to brown all sides. Add
the tomatoes and liquid, onion, Worcestershire sauce, garlic, bay leaf, sugar,
thyme and pepper. Simmer, covered, for 1 1/2 hours or until the beef is tender,
stirring occasionally. Add the potatoes, carrots, celery and hot water. Simmer,
covered, for 30 minutes or until the vegetables are tender-crisp, stirring
occasionally. Discard the bay leaf. Add salt to taste. Serve with rice or pasta.

■ ■ ■ ■ ■

LAMB STEW
Serves Six

4 cloves of garlic, minced
1 teaspoon salt
3 tablespoons cider vinegar
2 bay leaves
1/2 teaspoon pepper
2 pounds lamb, cut into cubes

2 medium yellow onions, cut into
  1-inch pieces
1/2 cup olive oil
1 (8-ounce) can tomato sauce
1 cup dry vermouth

Mash the garlic, salt and cider vinegar together in a bowl. Add the bay leaves
and pepper and mix well. Stir in the lamb cubes. Marinate, covered, in the
refrigerator for 1 to 3 hours. Drain, reserving the marinade. Sauté the onions
in 3 tablespoons of the olive oil in a large skillet until soft. Remove the onions
with a slotted spoon to a bowl. Pat the lamb cubes dry with paper towels. Add the
remaining olive oil to the skillet. Brown the lamb in the oil, turning to brown
all sides. Add the onions, the reserved marinade, tomato sauce and vermouth.
Simmer over low heat for 45 minutes or until the lamb is tender, stirring
occasionally. Serve with pasta or rice.

LOUISIANA VEAL STEW
Serves Eight

3 pounds veal cubes
¹/₂ cup canola oil
¹/₂ cup flour
1 tablespoon minced garlic
1 onion, chopped
³/₄ cup chopped green onions
   and tops
³/₄ cup chopped celery
1 cup chopped green bell pepper
¹/₂ cup crushed tomato

2 teaspoons salt
Freshly ground black pepper
¹/₂ teaspoon thyme
2 bay leaves
³/₄ cup water
³/₄ cup red wine
¹/₄ teaspoon Tabasco sauce
1¹/₂ tablespoons Worcestershire
   sauce
5 tablespoons chopped parsley

Brown the veal cubes in the canola oil in a large skillet, turning to brown all sides. Remove to a bowl with a slotted spoon. Stir the flour into the pan drippings. Cook over low heat for several minutes until dark brown, stirring constantly. Add the garlic, onion, green onions and tops, celery and green pepper. Sauté until the vegetables are limp. Add the tomato, salt and pepper. Simmer for 5 minutes, stirring constantly. Add the thyme, bay leaves, water, wine, Tabasco sauce and Worcestershire sauce and mix well. Add the veal cubes. Simmer for 1 hour, stirring occasionally. Discard the bay leaves. Stir in the parsley. Pour into a bowl. Chill, covered, for several hours to develop the flavor. Reheat just before serving. Serve with rice or mashed potatoes.

Ramona Measom was a surgical technician and upon a move to Charleston decided to pursue her real love, cooking. She is a graduate of Johnson and Wales Culinary Institute and has worked at Louis' Charleston Grill for Louis Osteen, one of America's premier chefs. She is currently working with Chef Louis Osteen in his new restaurant venture.

Ramona Measom's Plum Sweet-And-Sour Sauce
Serves Sixteen

1 (20-ounce) can crushed pineapple
   in heavy syrup
1 cup sugar
1 cup water
1 cup distilled vinegar

1 tablespoon dark soy sauce
2 tablespoons cornstarch
2 tablespoons cold water
1 cup plum sauce or plum jam

Combine the pineapple and syrup, sugar, 1 cup water, vinegar and soy sauce in a saucepan. Bring to a boil, stirring frequently. Stir the cornstarch into the cold water in a bowl, mixing well. Stir into the pineapple mixture. Bring to a boil over medium heat, stirring constantly. Pour into a bowl. Cool to room temperature. Stir in the plum sauce. Store, covered, in the refrigerator. Serve with egg rolls, baked chicken or ham. May freeze for later use. As a variation, substitute orange marmalade for the plum sauce.

. . . . .

Ramona Measom's Red Sweet-And-Sour Sauce
Serves Four

¹/₂ cup red wine vinegar
¹/₂ cup catsup

¹/₃ cup sugar
15 drops of red pepper sauce

Combine the vinegar, catsup, sugar and red pepper sauce in a bowl and mix until the sugar is dissolved. Store, covered, in the refrigerator.

THE POWDER MAGAZINE

Charleston was in dangerous isolation during the Colonial period, particularly during the War of the Spanish Succession (1701-1714), when England was in armed conflict with both Spain and France. As part of a program to strengthen the city's defenses, the Commons House of Assembly, in 1703, authorized the construction of the Powder Magazine, which was completed by 1713. The Magazine, located at 79 Cumberland Street, is the oldest public building in the Carolinas and is a relic of the time—circa 1704 to 1720 when Charleston was a walled city. The low square building is solidly constructed of brick, with a pantiled roof. It continued in use as a powder magazine until the American Revolution. Later, the building was used as a warehouse, and even a wine cellar. Subsequently, the property was acquired by the South Carolina Society of Colonial Dames of America. It is now a museum open to the public.

Poultry

D POWDER MAGAZINE
RELIC OF REVOLUTIONARY WAR
CHARLESTON, S. C.

POULTRY

CHEF ELIZABETH WARE'S ARROZ CON POLLO (CHICKEN WITH RICE)

Serves Four

1/4 cup tomato sauce
1 large green bell pepper, chopped
1 medium onion, chopped
2 cloves of garlic, minced
1/4 cup vegetable oil
1 (2-pound) chicken, cut up
1 tablespoon salt
1/2 teaspoon pepper

1 teaspoon bijol, or 1 tablespoon
   yellow food coloring
1 (12-ounce) can beer
1 cup water
2 cups uncooked rice
1 (8-ounce) can green peas
1 (4-ounce) can whole pimentos

Heat the tomato sauce, green pepper, onion, garlic and oil in a large ovenproof skillet. Add the chicken. Heat for several minutes. Add salt and pepper. Stir the bijol or food coloring into a small amount of water. Add to the chicken, mixing well. Add the beer, water, rice and undrained peas, mixing well. Reserve 1 pimento for garnish. Chop remaining pimentos. Add undrained pimentos to the chicken. Boil, covered, over high heat for 5 minutes. Bake, covered, at 325 degrees for 25 to 30 minutes or until chicken is cooked through. Spoon into a serving dish. Garnish with reserved pimento.

▪ ▪ ▪ ▪ ▪

Chef Elizabeth Ware took a trip with her family, when she was twelve, to visit Dr. Ernesto "Ernie" Toures Silvervestorini, a medical school friend of her dad's. This version of Arroz Con Pollo, which was served on her visit, was the first she ever had.

CHICKEN AND ARTICHOKE CASSEROLE
Serves Four

2 to 3 pounds chicken pieces
1½ teaspoons salt
¼ teaspoon pepper
½ teaspoon paprika
6 tablespoons margarine
1 (4-ounce) can mushroom pieces,
   drained

2 tablespoons flour
¼ cup sherry
¼ teaspoon rosemary
1⅓ cups chicken broth
1 (14-ounce) can artichoke hearts,
   drained

Sprinkle the chicken with salt, pepper and paprika. Brown the chicken in
4 tablespoons of the margarine in a skillet, turning to brown both sides.
Spoon into a greased baking dish using a slotted spoon. Add the remaining
2 tablespoons margarine to the pan drippings in the skillet. Add the mushrooms.
Sauté the mushrooms for several minutes. Sprinkle in the flour. Stir in the sherry,
rosemary and chicken broth. Cook for several minutes or until the sauce is
thickened, stirring constantly. Arrange the artichoke hearts around the chicken
in the baking dish. Pour the sauce over all. Bake, covered, at 375 degrees for
40 minutes or until the chicken is tender.

CHICKEN, ALMONDS AND PEACHES
Serves Eight

2/3 cup flour
1 1/2 teaspoons paprika
1 teaspoon salt
1/2 teaspoon ground black pepper
4 whole chicken breasts, split, skinned
1/2 cup corn oil

1 (29-ounce) can peach halves
1/2 cup slivered almonds
1 (10-ounce) can beef broth
2 tablespoons catsup
1 cup sour cream
1/2 cup grated Parmesan cheese

Combine 1/3 cup flour, paprika, salt and pepper in a shallow bowl and mix well. Roll the chicken in the mixture to coat. Brown the chicken in the oil in a large skillet over medium heat, turning to brown both sides. Remove to a greased baking dish using a slotted spoon. Drain the peaches, reserving the juice. Add enough water to the reserved juice to measure 1 1/2 cups liquid. Sauté the almonds in the pan drippings in the skillet until light brown. Stir in the remaining 1/3 cup flour. Add the peach juice mixture, broth and catsup, mixing well. Cook over low heat until thickened, stirring constantly. Remove from the heat. Stir in the sour cream. Pour over the chicken. Cover with foil. Bake at 350 degrees for 1 hour. Remove the foil. Arrange the peaches cut side up over the chicken; sprinkle with the Parmesan cheese. Bake, uncovered, for 10 minutes or until the chicken is cooked through. Serve with pasta or rice. Garnish with parsley.

Chicken Cacciatore
Serves Eight

8 boneless skinless chicken breast
   halves
$^1/_2$ cup olive oil
1 bunch green onions, chopped
1 cup chopped celery
3 teaspoons (heaping) minced
   ready-to-use garlic
1 (16-ounce) can peeled whole
   tomatoes

1 (4- to 6-ounce) jar sliced
   mushrooms, drained
1 (6-ounce) can tomato paste
1 tablespoon sugar
Salt and pepper to taste
$^1/_2$ cup dry sherry
1 (8-ounce) package spaghetti

Brown the chicken in the olive oil in a large skillet, turning to brown both sides. Remove the chicken to a bowl using a slotted spoon. Sauté the onions, celery and garlic in the pan drippings in the skillet over low heat for 15 minutes . Drain the tomatoes, reserving the juice. Coarsely chop the tomatoes. Add enough water to the reserved juice to measure 3 cups. Add the tomatoes, tomato juice mixture, mushrooms, tomato paste, sugar, salt, pepper and sherry to the skillet, mixing well. Add the chicken. Simmer, covered, over low heat for 1 to 2 hours or until the chicken is tender, stirring occasionally and adding additional water if the sauce becomes too thick. Cook the spaghetti using the package directions. Serve the sauce over the spaghetti with the chicken on the side.

CUMBERLAND STREET CHICKEN

Serves Eight

¹/₂ cup flour
1 teaspoon salt
¹/₄ teaspoon pepper
4 whole boneless chicken breasts,
    split
¹/₂ cup butter

¹/₄ cup minced green onions
¹/₄ cup chicken broth
³/₄ cup dry white wine
¹/₂ pound fresh mushrooms, sliced
2 cups seedless grapes

Combine the flour, salt and pepper in a shallow bowl and mix well. Roll the chicken in the mixture to coat. Brown the chicken in 5 tablespoons of the butter in a large skillet, turning to brown both sides. Remove the chicken using a slotted spoon and arrange close together in a greased baking dish. Sauté the onions in the pan drippings in a skillet just until tender. Stir in the broth and wine. Bring to a boil. Pour over the chicken. Bake, covered, at 350 degrees for 1 hour. Sauté the mushrooms in the remaining 3 tablespoons butter in a skillet. Add the mushrooms and grapes to the chicken. Bake, covered, for 10 minutes longer or just until the grapes are heated.

. . . . .

CHICKEN PIEMONTESE

Serves Four

4 boneless chicken breasts,
    pounded thin
Flour
1 (14-ounce) can artichoke
    bottoms or hearts, drained
¹/₄ cup butter

³/₄ cup vermouth or other white
    wine
³/₄ cup chicken bouillon
2 cups cream
Salt and white pepper to taste

Dredge the chicken in the flour in a bowl. Brown the chicken with the artichokes in the butter in a large skillet. Add the vermouth. Cook over medium heat until reduced by half, stirring frequently. Add the bouillon and cream. Cook over medium heat until partially reduced and the chicken is cooked through. Remove the chicken to a platter and keep warm in a 250-degree oven. Cook the sauce over medium heat until reduced by half, stirring frequently. Add the salt and white pepper. Pour the sauce over the chicken and serve.

ISLAND CURRIED CHICKEN
Serves Four

1 tablespoon (heaping) curry
  powder
Ground pepper, oregano, cloves,
  basil and garlic to taste
4 boneless chicken breasts
2 tablespoons vegetable oil

1 medium onion, chopped
1 medium tomato, chopped
1 small bell pepper, chopped
Salt to taste
4 cups hot cooked rice

Combine the curry powder, pepper, oregano, cloves, basil and garlic in a shallow bowl and mix well. Coat the chicken in the mixture. Brown the chicken in the oil in a large skillet for 15 minutes, turning to brown both sides. Add the onion, tomato, bell pepper and salt. Cook over medium heat for 5 minutes or until the chicken is cooked through, stirring frequently. Serve on a bed of rice in a serving dish.

• • • • •

HOMEMADE CURRY POWDER

1 tablespoon ground
  coriander
1 tablespoon black pepper
1 tablespoon cumin
1 tablespoon chili powder
1 tablespoon turmeric
3/4 teaspoon ground ginger

Combine all the ingredients in a bowl and mix well. Store in an airtight container.

CHICKEN WITH CASHEWS AND CREAM
Serves Eight

8 boneless skinless chicken breasts
1/3 cup butter
1 cup chopped onion
1 clove of garlic, minced
1/2 teaspoon salt
2 teaspoons ground ginger
1/4 teaspoon chili powder

1/2 cup drained canned tomatoes
1 cup chicken stock or plain yogurt
1/2 cup ground cashews
1/2 cup coconut
2 tablespoons cornstarch
1 cup heavy cream
Cooked rice

Cut the chicken breasts into quarters. Cook the chicken in the butter in a large skillet until cooked through, turning to brown all sides. Remove to a bowl using a slotted spoon. Sauté the onion and garlic in the pan drippings in the skillet for 5 minutes. Add the salt, ginger, chili powder, tomatoes and chicken stock. Cook for 15 minutes over low heat, stirring frequently. Add the cashews and coconut. Cook for 10 minutes, stirring frequently. Combine the cornstarch and heavy cream in a bowl and mix well. Add to the sauce. Cook over low heat until thickened, stirring constantly. Spoon the rice into a serving bowl. Add the chicken and cover with the sauce.

GREEK FETA CHICKEN
Serves Four

1 cup plain lowfat yogurt
1 tablespoon fresh lemon juice
$1/4$ to $1/2$ teaspoon dried oregano
$1/4$ to $1/2$ teaspoon dried rosemary
$1/4$ teaspoon pepper
1 large clove of garlic, minced

4 (4-ounce) boneless skinless
   chicken breasts
$1/3$ cup (or more) crumbled feta
   cheese
1 tablespoon chopped parsley

Combine the yogurt, lemon juice, oregano, rosemary, pepper and garlic in a sealable plastic bag. Add the chicken. Seal the bag and shake to coat the chicken with the mixture. Marinate, covered, in the refrigerator for 30 minutes or longer. Remove the chicken to the rack of a broiler pan coated with nonstick cooking spray, reserving the marinade. Broil $5^{1}/2$ inches from the heat source for 7 minutes with the oven door partially open. Turn over the chicken and spoon the reserved marinade over the chicken. Top with the feta cheese. Broil for 7 minutes longer or until the chicken is cooked through. Remove to a serving platter. Garnish with the parsley.

HOBCAW CHICKEN
Serves Six

$1/2$ cup plain yogurt
$3/4$ teaspoon hot sauce
$1/2$ teaspoon salt
1 tablespoon Dijon mustard

3 pounds chicken pieces
$2^{1}/2$ cups bread crumbs
$1/4$ teaspoon cayenne pepper
3 tablespoons vegetable oil

Combine the yogurt, hot sauce, salt and mustard in a shallow bowl and mix well. Add the chicken and stir until coated. Marinate, covered, in the refrigerator for 8 to 10 hours. Mix the bread crumbs and cayenne pepper together. Roll each piece of chicken in the crumb mixture until coated. Place in a foil-lined baking dish. Drizzle with the oil. Bake at 400 degrees for 1 hour. Serve hot or cold.

Hunter's Chicken
Serves Four

4 large skinless chicken breasts
1 envelope Italian salad dressing
  mix
3 tablespoons olive oil
4 green onions and tops, sliced
1 large package fresh mushrooms,
  thinly sliced

3 tablespoons butter
1 (28-ounce) can tomatoes
2 teaspoons tarragon
1 small bottle (4-pack size) white
  wine

Sprinkle the chicken with ¹/₂ of the dressing mix, reserving the remaining mix. Brown the chicken in the olive oil in a large skillet over high heat, turning to brown both sides. Remove the chicken to a bowl and discard the oil. Sauté the onions and mushrooms in the butter in the same skillet, scraping the bottom of the skillet. Drain the tomatoes, reserving ¹/₂ of the liquid. Coarsely chop the tomatoes. Add the tomatoes and reserved liquid, tarragon, wine and reserved dressing mix to the skillet and mix well. Return the chicken to the skillet. Cook over low to medium heat for 1 hour or until the chicken is tender, stirring occasionally. Serve the chicken and sauce with rice or pasta.

■ ■ ■ ■ ■

Rosemary Garlic Chicken
Serves Twenty

1 cup fresh rosemary needles,
  all stems removed
10 cloves of garlic, peeled
1 tablespoon salt

1¹/₂ teaspoons black pepper
3 to 4 tablespoons olive oil
10 whole chicken breasts

Rinse the rosemary and pat dry. Combine the rosemary, garlic, salt and pepper in a food processor. Process until coarsely chopped. Add 2 tablespoons of the olive oil. Process until a coarse paste forms. Add the remaining olive oil. Process until well mixed. Spread the paste on the chicken. Chill, covered, for 6 hours or longer. Cook the chicken on a hot grill. Watch closely to prevent the rosemary burning.

CHICKEN WITH LEMON SAUCE
Serves Four

$^1/_2$ cup flour
$^1/_4$ teaspoon pepper
1 teaspoon salt

$2^1/_2$ to 3 pounds chicken, cut up
$^1/_2$ cup melted butter or margarine
Lemon Sauce

Combine the flour, pepper and salt in a shallow bowl. Rinse the chicken and pat dry. Roll the chicken in the flour mixture to coat. Arrange skin side down in a shallow baking dish. Drizzle with melted butter. Bake at 400 degrees for 30 minutes. Turn over the chicken. Pour the Lemon Sauce over the chicken. Bake for 30 minutes longer or until golden brown and tender. Remove to a serving platter. Garnish with lemon slices.

LEMON SAUCE

$^1/_2$ tablespoon soy sauce
$^1/_2$ teaspoon salt
$^1/_2$ teaspoon pepper

$^1/_4$ cup vegetable oil
$^1/_2$ cup fresh lemon juice
1 clove of garlic, minced

Combine the soy sauce, salt, pepper, oil, lemon juice and garlic in a bowl and mix well.

East Indian Chicken
Serves Eight

1/4 cup soy sauce
2 tablespoons olive oil
1 teaspoon ground ginger
2 cloves of garlic, minced
1 tablespoon lemon juice
1 teaspoon ground coriander

1/2 teaspoon ground cumin
1/4 teaspoon ground cardamom
1/4 teaspoon turmeric
1/8 to 1/4 teaspoon cayenne pepper
8 boneless skinless chicken breasts

Combine the soy sauce, olive oil, ginger, garlic, lemon juice, coriander, cumin, cardamom, turmeric and cayenne pepper in a resealable plastic bag. Seal the bag and shake to mix the seasonings. Add the chicken; seal and shake the bag to coat the chicken. Marinate, covered, in the refrigerator for 4 to 24 hours. Cook on a hot grill for about 20 minutes or until the chicken juices run clear. Serve with rice pilaf and cucumber salad.

■　■　■　■

Oriental Chicken Kabobs
Serves Eight

3 tablespoons soy sauce
3 tablespoons Italian salad dressing
2 teaspoons sesame seeds
2 teaspoons lemon juice
1/4 teaspoon ground ginger
1 clove of garlic, minced
3 chicken breast halves

1 small green bell pepper, cut
　into eighths
1 small onion, cut into eighths
1 (14-ounce) can artichoke hearts,
　drained
8 cherry tomatoes

Combine the soy sauce, salad dressing, sesame seeds, lemon juice, ginger and garlic in a bowl and mix well. Cut the chicken into 1-inch pieces and place in a shallow dish. Pour the soy sauce mixture over the chicken. Marinate, covered, in the refrigerator for 2 hours or longer. Drain the chicken, reserving the marinade. Thread the chicken, green pepper, onion, artichoke hearts and cherry tomatoes alternately onto 8 skewers. Grill until the chicken is cooked through, basting with the reserved marinade. May also be cooked in a microwave but do not add the tomatoes until near the end of the cooking time.

MORRIS ISLAND STICKY ROAST CHICKEN
Serves Six

2 teaspoons salt
1 teaspoon paprika
³/₄ teaspoon cayenne pepper
¹/₂ teaspoon onion powder
¹/₂ teaspoon thyme

¹/₄ teaspoon white pepper
¹/₄ teaspoon garlic powder
¹/₄ teaspoon black pepper
1 (3-pound) chicken
1 cup chopped onions

Combine the salt, paprika, cayenne pepper, onion powder, thyme, white pepper, garlic powder and black pepper in a bowl and mix well. Rub the mixture over the chicken inside and out, rubbing deeply into the skin. Place the chicken in a sealable plastic bag. Marinate in the refrigerator for 8 to 10 hours. Remove the chicken from the plastic bag. Fill the cavity of the chicken with the chopped onions. Place in a roasting pan. Roast at 250 degrees for 5 hours, basting with the pan drippings occasionally.

■　■　■　■　■

CRANBERRY CHUTNEY
Serves Eight

1 pound cranberries
1 cup sugar
¹/₂ cup packed brown sugar
2 teaspoons ground cinnamon
1¹/₂ teaspoons ground ginger

¹/₂ teaspoon ground cloves
¹/₄ teaspoon allspice
1 cup water
¹/₂ cup golden raisins
1 cup chopped peeled apple

Rinse the cranberries and discard blemished cranberries. Combine the cranberries, sugar, brown sugar, cinnamon, ginger, cloves, allspice and water in a saucepan and mix well. Cook over medium heat for 15 minutes or until the juice is released, stirring frequently. Reduce the heat to low. Add the raisins and apple. Simmer, uncovered, for 15 minutes or until thickened, stirring frequently. Cool in the refrigerator.

SESAME CHICKEN
Serves Four

3 boneless skinless chicken breasts
1 cup sour cream
2 tablespoons lemon juice
2 teaspoons celery seeds
2 teaspoons Worcestershire sauce
$^1/_2$ teaspoon salt

$^1/_4$ teaspoon pepper
2 cloves of garlic, minced
1 cup bread crumbs
$^1/_3$ cup sesame seeds
$^1/_4$ cup melted margarine

Cut the chicken into strips and place in a shallow dish. Combine the sour cream, lemon juice, celery seeds, Worcestershire sauce, salt, pepper and garlic in a bowl and mix well. Pour over the chicken. Marinate, covered, in the refrigerator for 8 to 10 hours. Combine the bread crumbs and sesame seeds in a shallow bowl. Roll the chicken strips in the mixture to coat and place on a greased baking sheet. Drizzle with the melted margarine. Bake at 350 degrees for 35 to 40 minutes or until the chicken is cooked through.

■ ■ ■ ■ ■

BAKED ROSEMARY CHICKEN

Stuff the cavity of a whole chicken with rosemary branches and roast as usual. If using chicken breasts, gently disconnect the skin from the chicken breasts. Stuff the rosemary branches under the chicken skin and bake as usual. Discard the rosemary after baking.

POLLO FORTE
Serves Six

$^1/_2$ cup olive oil plus 1 teaspoon anchovy oil
8 anchovy fillets, mashed
$1^1/_2$ teaspoons flour
$1^1/_2$ cups chicken broth
1 (4-ounce) jar pimentos, drained

2 cloves of garlic, minced
Salt and pepper to taste
2 tablespoons strong white vinegar
1 jar capers
1 chicken, boiled, deboned, coarsely chopped

Heat the oil in a saucepan over medium heat; add the mashed anchovy fillets. Mix until well blended. Stir in the flour, mixing well. Add the broth, pimentos and garlic and mix well. Bring to a boil. Cook for 10 minutes, stirring constantly. Pour into a blender container. Process until puréed. Return to the saucepan. Add the salt and pepper. Simmer over low heat for 10 minutes longer. Remove from the heat. Stir in the vinegar and capers. Pour over the chopped chicken in a bowl; mix well. Chill, covered, in the refrigerator for 8 to 10 hours before serving.

LEMON CHICKEN LEGARE
Serves Eight

1/2 cup flour
1 teaspoon salt
1 teaspoon paprika
8 boneless skinless chicken
 breast halves
Juice of 3 lemons
3 tablespoons (or more) olive oil

1 cube chicken bouillon
3/4 cup boiling water
2 tablespoons brown sugar
1/4 cup chopped green onions and
 tops
Fresh parsley
Lemon slices

Combine the flour, salt and paprika in a plastic bag, mixing well. Combine the chicken and lemon juice in a bowl. Let stand for 10 to 15 minutes. Remove the chicken, reserving the lemon juice. Add the chicken 1 piece at a time to the plastic bag, shaking to coat with the flour mixture. Cook the chicken in the oil in a skillet over medium-high heat, turning to brown both sides and cooking through. Remove the chicken to a platter, reserving the pan drippings. Keep the chicken warm in a 150-degree oven. Dissolve the bouillon cube in the boiling water in a bowl. Stir in the brown sugar and reserved lemon juice. Pour into the pan drippings in the skillet. Bring to a boil, stirring frequently. Reduce the heat to low. Simmer, covered, for 5 minutes or until thickened, stirring occasionally. Add the onions. Simmer, covered, for 10 minutes, stirring occasionally. Place the chicken on a serving platter. Pour the sauce over the chicken. Garnish with the parsley and lemon slices.

■ ■ ■ ■ ■

CHICKEN WITH MARINADE DEWEES
Serves Six

1/2 cup packed brown sugar
1/3 cup vegetable oil
1/4 cup cider vinegar
3 cloves of garlic, minced

3 tablespoons coarse grain mustard
1 1/2 tablespoons lemon or lime juice
6 chicken breast halves

Combine the brown sugar, oil, cider vinegar, garlic, mustard and lemon juice in a shallow bowl and mix well. Add the chicken, turning to coat both sides. Marinate, covered, in the refrigerator for 2 hours or longer. Cook on a hot grill until the chicken is cooked through.

Seabrook Tetrazzini

Serves Six

1 chicken
3 (10-ounce) cans chicken broth
1 pound fresh mushrooms, sliced
1 green bell pepper, chopped
1 clove of garlic, minced
$1/4$ cup butter
3 tablespoons flour
$1^3/4$ cups (or more) half-and-half

$1/4$ cup dry white wine
Salt and pepper to taste
2 egg yolks, slightly beaten
8 to 10 ounces uncooked vermicelli
   or linguini pasta
2 small bay leaves
Freshly grated Parmesan cheese

Combine the chicken and the chicken broth in a large saucepan, adding water to cover the chicken if needed. Cook until the chicken is very tender. Remove the chicken, reserving the broth. Remove the skin and bones and chop the chicken. Strain the broth and reserve. Sauté the mushrooms, green pepper and garlic in the butter in a large skillet. Stir in the flour until well mixed. Stir in $1^1/2$ to 2 cups of the reserved broth and the half-and-half gradually. Cook over low heat for 5 minutes or until thickened, stirring constantly. Add the wine, salt and pepper and mix well. Add a small amount of the sauce to the egg yolks. Stir the egg yolks into the sauce. Add the chopped chicken and heat. Cook the pasta with the bay leaves in boiling water in a large saucepan using the package directions. Discard the bay leaves. Drain the pasta and place in a buttered casserole. Spoon the chicken and sauce over the pasta. Sprinkle generously with Parmesan cheese. Bake at 350 degrees for 30 to 35 minutes or until heated through.

Spicy Chicken Quesadillas
Serves Five

4 boneless skinless chicken breast halves
1 envelope taco seasoning mix
2½ cups shredded Monterey Jack cheese

⅔ cup picante sauce
1 medium red bell pepper, chopped
10 (10-inch) flour tortillas
Melted butter

Cut the chicken into ¼-inch strips. Combine the chicken and the taco seasoning mix in a sealable plastic bag. Seal the bag; shake to coat the chicken. Marinate in the refrigerator for 1 hour. Arrange the chicken in a 10x15-inch baking pan. Broil the chicken under a hot broiler with the oven door partially open for 5 minutes or until cooked through. Cool the chicken and cut into bite-size pieces. Combine the chicken, cheese, picante sauce and red pepper in a bowl and mix well. Brush 1 side of each tortilla with melted butter. Place half of the tortillas buttered side down on 2 baking sheets. Top the tortillas with 1 cup of the chicken mixture, spreading to the edges of the tortillas. Place the remaining tortillas buttered side up over the chicken mixture. Bake at 375 degrees for 10 minutes or until golden brown. Cut into wedges. May cook the quesadillas 1 at a time in a cast-iron skillet or on a griddle on top of the stove for 3 minutes on each side.

LOWCOUNTRY CRAB-STUFFED CHICKEN
Serves Eight

8 boneless skinless chicken breast
   halves
¹/₄ cup butter
¹/₄ cup flour
³/₄ cup milk
³/₄ cup chicken broth
¹/₃ cup dry white wine
¹/₄ cup chopped onion
¹/₃ cup sliced fresh mushrooms, or
   1 (3-ounce) can mushroom,
   drained

8 ounces fresh crab meat, or
   1 (7-ounce) can crab meat,
   drained, flaked
10 saltine crackers, crumbled
2 tablespoons chopped fresh parsley
¹/₂ teaspoon salt
Pepper to taste
1 cup grated Swiss cheese
¹/₂ teaspoon paprika

Place the chicken between sheets of waxed paper. Pound the chicken with a meat mallet until ¹/₈ inch thick. Melt 3 tablespoons of the butter in a saucepan. Stir in the flour. Add the milk, broth and wine, mixing well. Simmer over low heat until thickened, stirring constantly. Sauté the onion and mushrooms in the remaining 1 tablespoon butter in a large skillet. Stir in the crab meat, cracker crumbs, parsley, salt, pepper and 2 tablespoons of the sauce. Top each piece of chicken with a portion of the crab meat mixture. Roll the chicken to enclose the filling, sealing with a wooden pick. Place in a greased baking dish. Spread the remaining sauce over the chicken. Bake, covered, at 350 degrees for 1 hour. Sprinkle with the Swiss cheese and paprika. Bake for 5 minutes longer or until the cheese melts.

INTERNATIONAL FARE

MOROCCAN CORNISH GAME HENS
Serves Four

4 Cornish game hens
2 large lemons, cut into halves
4 large cloves of garlic, peeled
1$^{1}/_{2}$ teaspoons salt
1 tablespoon paprika

2 teaspoons ground cumin
$^{1}/_{4}$ cup olive oil
$^{1}/_{4}$ to $^{1}/_{2}$ cup orange marmalade
   or honey

Split the hens along the back and open flat. Place skin side up in a roasting pan. Squeeze the juice from $^{1}/_{2}$ lemon over each hen. Place the squeezed lemon under the hen. Combine the garlic, salt, paprika, cumin, olive oil and marmalade in a food processor. Process until of a paste-like consistency. Spread the mixture over the hens to coat. Bake at 400 degrees for 50 to 55 minutes or until the hens are cooked through, basting frequently with the pan drippings and adding additional liquid if the pan drippings become dry.

• • • • •

TURKEY-SPINACH-BLEU CHEESEBURGERS
Serves Eight

1 pound ground turkey
1 (10-ounce) package frozen
   chopped spinach, thawed

Crumbled bleu cheese or feta cheese
   to taste

Combine the turkey, spinach and cheese in a bowl and mix well. Let stand, covered, in the refrigerator for 1 hour to meld the flavors. Shape into patties. Cook on a hot grill sprayed with nonstick cooking spray until cooked through. Serve with lettuce, tomato and red onion. Good served with red potato chunks seasoned with Greek seasoning and sprayed with olive oil-flavored nonstick cooking spray. Bake the potatoes at 400 degrees for 45 minutes or until golden brown.

The Mosquito Fleet

West Africans brought with them to the South Carolina Lowcountry a tradition of fishing. Fishnets, made and used by Lowcountry fishermen, are identical to those made by their kinsmen across the Atlantic. During the eighteenth and nineteenth centuries, water-related occupations (boatmen, fishermen, etc.) were the main pursuits of African-Americans.

The Mosquito Fleet was a group of boats of varying sizes and types owned and employed by black entrepreneurs. They fished in the Lowcountry waters and bravely ventured out into the Atlantic, often in small vessels. The dangers inherent in such a lifestyle were tragically illustrated when the Mosquito Fleet was wiped out by a hurricane in 1940. The survivors rebuilt, but the competition of the larger, more expensive commercial trawlers eventually put the Mosquito Fleet out of business. This early twentieth-century view was taken by Bayard Wooten, a Charleston photographer.

Seafood

QUITO FLEET, CHARLESTON, S. C.

—*Photo by Bayard Wooten*

SEAFOOD

Trawler's Piquante Swordfish Steaks And Fresh Herbs

Serves Four

4 (8-ounce) swordfish steaks,
   1 inch thick
1/4 cup chopped fresh coriander
1/4 cup chopped fresh parsley
2 cloves of garlic, minced
1/2 teaspoon ground coriander

1/4 teaspoon ground cumin
Pinch of cayenne pepper
Juice of 2 limes or lemons
3 tablespoons olive oil
Salt and black pepper to taste

Pat the swordfish dry with paper towels. Combine the fresh coriander, parsley, garlic, ground coriander, cumin and cayenne pepper in a food processor. Process until blended. Add the lime juice and olive oil, processing constantly until smooth. Spread the herb mixture onto both sides of the swordfish. Place in a shallow dish. Marinate, covered, in the refrigerator for 1 hour. Remove the swordfish from the marinade. Season with salt and black pepper. Cook on a hot grill for 4 to 5 minutes on each side or just until opaque throughout.

■ ■ ■ ■ ■

Shrimping and fishing has always been a way of life and a major industry along the Carolina coast. Mt. Pleasant is home base to shrimping fleets called trawlers. Trawlers are boats geared for dragging their nets on the ocean floor, then pulling in the haul. The trawlers dock at Shem Creek and prepare their catch for market. In 1967, The Trawler Restaurant opened, offering fresh, local seafood and a picturesque view of Shem Creek lined with trawlers festooned with nets that bring home their bounteous catch.

Today, The Trawler Restaurant is owned by Horst Semper who continues the tradition of serving fresh local seafood on scenic Shem Creek.

Fillet Of Flounder On Bed Of Mushrooms

Serves Four

1 pound fresh mushrooms
2 shallots, peeled, finely chopped
1/4 cup butter
Salt, black pepper and nutmeg
   to taste
1 1/2 pounds fillet of flounder
1/2 cup dry white wine
1/2 cup cold water
8 black peppercorns

1 bay leaf
Juice of 1 lemon, strained
1/4 cup butter
2 tablespoons flour
1/2 cup heavy cream
1/4 teaspoon nutmeg
1/8 teaspoon cayenne pepper
1 tablespoon chopped parsley

Rinse the mushrooms and pat dry. Remove the tough part of the stems and discard. Chop the mushrooms finely. Sauté the shallots in 1/4 cup butter in a skillet over low heat for 3 minutes. Do not brown. Add the mushrooms. Cook over low heat for 5 minutes, stirring frequently. Sprinkle with salt, black pepper and nutmeg. Rinse the flounder and pat dry. Place in a buttered 10x16-inch baking dish. Add the wine, cold water, peppercorns, bay leaf and lemon juice. Dot with 2 tablespoons of the butter. Bake at 350 degrees for 25 minutes or until the flounder is opaque. Discard the bay leaf. Drain and reserve the liquid. Layer the mushrooms and flounder in a buttered 10x16-inch baking dish. Keep warm while making the sauce. Melt the remaining 2 tablespoons butter in a saucepan. Stir in the flour. Cook for 1 or 2 minutes, stirring constantly. Stir in the reserved liquid from the flounder. Cook until thickened, stirring constantly. Remove from heat. Stir in the heavy cream. Season with salt, black pepper, 1/4 teaspoon nutmeg and cayenne pepper. Pour over the flounder. Cook under a hot broiler in a 450-degree oven until the flounder is slightly brown. Sprinkle with the parsley. Serve at once.

Trawler's Salmon In Cucumber Sauce
Serves Four

1 onion, finely chopped
1 clove of garlic, minced
1/4 cup olive oil or butter
1 cup heavy cream
1 cup dry white wine
2 tablespoons brandy
2 tablespoons cider or white wine
   vinegar
2 tablespoons Dijon mustard

Salt and pepper to taste
2 large cucumbers, peeled
Chopped parsley
Chopped fresh dill
4 (7- to 8-ounce) salmon fillets,
   not steaks
1 teaspoon olive oil
White wine
Lemon juice

Sauté the onion and garlic in 1/4 cup oil in a large skillet until soft but not brown. Add the cream, white wine, brandy, cider vinegar, mustard, salt and pepper. Cook over high heat until thickened, stirring constantly. Cut the cucumbers into halves lengthwise. Remove the seeds and slice. Add the cucumber slices to the sauce. Cook over low heat until the cucumbers are soft. Add parsley and dill. Remove from the heat and keep warm. Preheat the oven to 400 degrees. Brown the salmon in 1 teaspoon olive oil in an ovenproof skillet for 1 minute. Turn the salmon. Bake in a 400-degree oven for 6 minutes. Sprinkle with a dash of white wine and lemon juice. Remove the salmon to a serving plate, spooning the wine mixture over the salmon. Garnish with parsley and dill. Serve with the cucumber sauce.

■ ■ ■ ■ ■

The Trawler is located on relaxing Shem Creek. Owner
Horst Semper has continued the thirty-year tradition of serving fresh
local seafood dishes that tantalize every taste.

Herb Wash For Seafood And Meat

¹/₂ to ³/₄ cup olive oil
Juice of 1 lemon
1 tablespoon each basil,
    thyme and rosemary

Combine the olive oil and lemon juice in a bowl and mix well. Stir in the basil, thyme and rosemary. Chill, covered, in the refrigerator for 8 to 10 hours. Baste the seafood or meat with the mixture while cooking on a grill. May substitute 1 tablespoon each dill and parsley for the herbs. May add 1 or 2 cloves of garlic, minced; 1 tablespoon spicy mustard; and/or 1 teaspoon fresh ground pepper. May substitute lime juice for lemon or reduce the amount of oil and increase the amount of juice. For more pronounced flavor, pour the mixture over the seafood or meat and marinate, covered, in the refrigerator for 8 to 10 hours.

Boone Hall Salmon
Serves Eight

1 tablespoon chopped parsley
1 tablespoon thyme
1 tablespoon chopped dill
1 (2¹/₂ pounds) salmon fillet
¹/₂ cup lemon juice
¹/₂ cup dry white wine
1 carrot, coarsely chopped
1 lemon, cut into halves
1 onion, coarsely chopped
1 rib celery, coarsely chopped
¹/₂ cup sour cream
2 tablespoons mayonnaise
2 tablespoons mustard

Combine the parsley, thyme and dill in a bowl and mix well. Place the salmon in a deep baking dish. Rub the seasoning mixture on the salmon. Pour in the lemon juice and wine. Add the carrot, lemon, onion and celery. Bake, covered, at 300 degrees for 20 minutes, watching closely to be sure it does not dry out. Combine the sour cream, mayonnaise and mustard in a bowl and mix well. Serve the sauce with the salmon.

· · · · ·

Garlic Dill Salmon
Serves Four

1 teaspoon vinegar
2 pounds salmon fillets
¹/₂ lemon
1 teaspoon garlic powder
¹/₂ cup clarified butter or margarine
Dash of ground cloves
Ground dillweed

Add the vinegar to enough water in a bowl to cover the salmon. Soak the salmon for 3 minutes. Drain and pat dry with paper towels. Squeeze the juice of the ¹/₂ lemon over the salmon. Turn on the oven broiler. Clarify the butter by heating in a skillet and removing the impurities which float to the top. Stir the garlic powder into the butter. Dip the salmon in the butter mixture to coat on all sides.Sprinkle with cloves and dillweed. Place on a rack in a broiler pan skin side up. Broil for 10 minutes. Turn the salmon; baste with the butter mixture. Broil for 5 minutes longer. Do not overcook. Serve with your favorite vegetables. Garnish with lemon slices.

SALMON PAPILLOTES
Serves Four

1/4 cup butter, softened, or olive oil
1/2 pound spinach, coarsely chopped
1 to 1 1/2 pounds skinless salmon
   fillets
2 tomatoes, peeled, seeded, chopped

1/2 cup fresh basil, chopped
1/4 cup milk
1/8 teaspoon white pepper
Salt to taste

Place 4 sheets of 16-inch long heavy-duty foil on a flat surface. Spread the butter over the surface to prevent sticking. Arrange 1/8 of the spinach in the center of each sheet of foil. Cut the salmon into 4 pieces. Layer 1 piece of the salmon, 1/4 of the tomatoes, 1/4 of the remaining spinach and 2 tablespoons basil on each serving of spinach. Add 1 tablespoon milk, some of the pepper and salt to each serving. Fold the foil to enclose, double folding the edges to seal. Place the packets on a baking sheet. Bake at 450 degrees for 12 to 15 minutes or until the salmon is done to taste.

■　■　■　■　■

MUSTARD CHIVE SALMON
Serves Four

3/4 cup butter, softened
3 1/2 tablespoons lemon juice
3 tablespoons chopped chives or
   green onions
1 1/2 tablespoons Dijon mustard

1 1/2 teaspoons grated lemon peel
3/4 teaspoon salt
1/4 teaspoon ground pepper
4 salmon or mahimahi fillets
4 teaspoons lemon juice

Combine the butter, 3 1/2 tablespoons lemon juice, chives, mustard, lemon peel, salt and pepper in a bowl and mix well. Arrange 1 large sheet of heavy-duty foil on a baking sheet. Spread 1 tablespoon of the mustard and chive mixture over the foil. Place the salmon skin side down on the foil. Add 1 teaspoon lemon juice to each piece of salmon; top with 1 tablespoon of the mustard and chive mixture. Bake at 450 degrees for 10 minutes. The butter mixture may also be served on fresh steamed vegetables.

Pesto Sauce

$^1/_2$ cup fresh basil leaves
    (about 15 with stems
    removed), or 2 teaspoons
    dried
$^1/_2$ cup parsley leaves
$^1/_2$ cup grated Parmesan
    cheese
$^1/_3$ cup pine nuts or walnuts
2 to 4 cloves of garlic,
    minced
$^1/_4$ to $^1/_2$ cup olive oil

Combine the basil, parsley, Parmesan cheese, pine nuts and garlic in a blender or food processor. Process until puréed. Add the oil in a slow steady stream until the mixture is paste-like, processing constantly. About half of this mixture is used in the Spinach Sole. Wrap the remaining sauce tightly and freeze for another use.

Shem Creek Sole With Pesto Sauce
Serves Four

4 (6- to 7-ounce) sole (flounder) or
    whiting fillets
Salt and pepper to taste
$^1/_2$ cup dry white wine or vermouth
1 tablespoon lemon juice
2 cloves of garlic, minced
1 small onion, chopped

2 tablespoons butter
2 bunches fresh spinach
$^3/_4$ cup grated Parmesan cheese
$^1/_2$ teaspoon dried oregano, or
    1 teaspoon fresh
1 cup sour cream
$^1/_4$ cup Pesto Sauce (at left)

Pat the sole dry with paper towels. Arrange in a single layer in a 9x13-inch baking dish. Sprinkle with salt and pepper. Pour in the wine and lemon juice. Bake, covered, at 400 degrees for 10 to 15 minutes or until the sole loses its translucency. Drain the liquid into a measuring cup and reserve. Cool the sole. Pour the reserved liquid into a saucepan and reduce over medium-high heat to $^1/_2$ to $^2/_3$ cup if liquid measures more than this amount. Cool the liquid. Sauté the garlic and onion in butter in a skillet over medium heat just until golden brown. Remove from the heat and cool slightly. Stir in the spinach, $^1/_2$ cup of the Parmesan cheese, oregano, salt and pepper, mixing well. The mixture will be thick. Divide the spinach mixture evenly over the sole fillets. Add the sour cream and $^1/_4$ cup Pesto Sauce to the reduced liquid. Season with salt and pepper. Spoon the mixture over the spinach mixture. Sprinkle with the remaining $^1/_4$ cup Parmesan cheese. Bake, uncovered, at 350 degrees for 5 to 10 minutes or until bubbly and the cheese is melted. May be refrigerated, covered, before the final baking.

TERIYAKI TUNA
Serves Eight

1/2 cup soy sauce
1/2 cup white wine
1 tablespoon lemon juice
1/4 cup vegetable oil

1 clove of garlic, minced
2 tablespoons sugar
8 tuna or swordfish fillets

Combine the soy sauce, wine, lemon juice, oil, garlic and sugar in a bowl and mix well. Arrange the tuna fillets in a shallow dish. Pour the marinade over the tuna. Marinate, covered, in the refrigerator for 2 to 4 hours. Cook on a grill.

. . . . .

BEER MARINADE FOR TUNA

12 ounces beer
1/2 cup olive oil
1/2 cup soy sauce
2 tablespoons chopped garlic

Combine the beer, olive oil, soy sauce and garlic in a bowl and mix well. Place the tuna in a shallow dish. Pour the marinade over the tuna. Marinate, covered, in the refrigerator for 30 to 60 minutes. Cook the tuna on a grill.

BLUE CRAB SOUFFLÉ
Serves Ten

1 pound crab meat
1 cup chopped celery
2 teaspoons onion juice, or 1 small onion, grated
2 teaspoons prepared mustard
1/2 cup mayonnaise
Tabasco sauce to taste

Lemon juice to taste
12 slices bread, crust removed
Melted butter
Grated sharp Cheddar cheese
5 eggs, slightly beaten
2 cups milk

Combine the crab meat, celery, onion juice, mustard, mayonnaise, Tabasco sauce and lemon juice in a bowl and mix well. Dip the bread in the melted butter. Make 6 sandwiches using the crab mixture as filling. Cut the sandwiches into fourths. Layer the sandwiches and cheese in a buttered 9x13-inch baking dish, making 2 layers of each. Beat the eggs and milk together. Pour over the layers. Cover; chill for 2 hours to overnight in the refrigerator. Place the baking dish in a large pan half filled with water. Bake at 325 degrees for 1 hour. May substitute chicken for the crab meat.

Scallops With Vegetables
Serves Four

2 onions, coarsely chopped
3 ribs celery, diagonally sliced
8 ounces green beans, diagonally
   sliced
2 teaspoons grated fresh gingerroot
1 clove of garlic, minced
2 tablespoons vegetable oil
4 teaspoons cornstarch
1 cup water

2½ tablespoons dry sherry
4 teaspoons instant chicken
   bouillon
2 tablespoons soy sauce
1 pound scallops
8 ounces mushrooms, sliced
6 green onions, sliced

Stir-fry the onions, celery, green beans, gingerroot and garlic in the oil in a wok over high heat for 3 minutes. Blend the cornstarch and 2 tablespoons of the water in a bowl. Blend in the remaining water, sherry, chicken bouillon and soy sauce. Stir into the vegetables. Cook until thickened, stirring constantly. Add the scallops, mushrooms and green onions. Cook for 4 minutes or just until the scallops are tender, stirring constantly.

• • • • •

Greek-Style Shrimp
Serves Two

1 medium onion, finely chopped
½ medium green bell pepper,
   chopped
1 to 3 cloves of garlic, minced
2 tablespoons olive oil
1 (28-ounce) can plum tomatoes
¾ teaspoon salt
½ teaspoon pepper

Juice of ½ lemon
¼ cup retsina or white wine
   (optional)
⅔ pound medium or large shrimp,
   peeled, deveined
2 tablespoons chopped parsley
4 ounces feta cheese, cubed
2 cups hot cooked rice

Sauté the onion, green pepper and garlic in the olive oil in a large skillet. Coarsely chop the tomatoes. Add tomatoes and juice, salt, pepper and lemon juice to the skillet. Simmer over low heat for 20 minutes or until thickened, stirring frequently. Stir in the wine. Return the mixture to a strong simmer. Add the shrimp and parsley. Cook for 3 to 5 minutes, stirring frequently. Remove from the heat. Add the cheese and toss gently to mix. Pour over hot rice in a serving bowl.

ALBEMARLE POINTE SHRIMP PILAF
Serves Four

1 cup uncooked rice
1/2 cup chopped celery
2 tablespoons chopped
  bell pepper
3 tablespoons butter or
  margarine
1 pound medium shrimp,
  peeled, deveined
1 teaspoon Worcestershire
  sauce
1 tablespoon flour
Salt and pepper to taste
Soy sauce to taste
Bacon bits

Cook the rice using the package
directions. Sauté the celery
and bell pepper in the butter in
a large skillet. Sprinkle the
shrimp with the Worcestershire
sauce. Roll in the flour in a bowl
until coated. Add to the skillet.
Sauté until the shrimp are
cooked. Season with salt,
pepper and soy sauce. Stir in
the cooked rice and mix well.
May add additional butter. Pour
into a serving bowl. Garnish
with bacon bits.

COOPER RIVER SHRIMP CREOLE
Serves Ten

2 cups chopped celery and leaves
2 green bell peppers, chopped
2 very large onions, chopped
1/2 cup olive oil
1 cup golden raisins
1 cup chili sauce
1 teaspoon sugar
2 (14-ounce) cans tomatoes
1 teaspoon curry powder
3 large bay leaves
1 cup white wine
5 pounds medium shrimp, cooked,
  peeled, deveined
Salt to taste
Cooked white rice

Sauté the celery, green peppers and onions in the olive oil in a saucepan. Add
the raisins, chili sauce, sugar, tomatoes, curry powder, bay leaves and wine
and mix well. Simmer, covered, for 30 minutes, stirring occasionally. Add the
shrimp. Heat to serving temperature. Discard the bay leaves. Season with salt.
Serve over rice.

. . . . .

GRATIN OF JUMBO SHRIMP
Serves Four

2/3 pound fresh mushrooms
Lemon juice
3 pounds jumbo shrimp, peeled,
  deveined
1/2 cup butter
3 cups heavy whipping cream
Nutmeg to taste
Cayenne pepper to taste
1/2 cup grated Gruyère or
  Emmentaler cheese

Sprinkle the mushrooms with lemon juice. Sauté the mushrooms and shrimp
in the butter in a large skillet for 3 to 5 minutes or until the shrimp are pink,
shaking the pan frequently. Remove the shrimp and mushrooms to a buttered
baking dish. Add the cream, nutmeg and cayenne pepper to the pan drippings.
Heat the cream, stirring constantly. Pour over the shrimp and mushrooms.
Sprinkle with the cheese and additional nutmeg. Broil for 5 to 6 minutes or until
brown. Serve with a Muscadet wine.

THE OLD POST OFFICE'S SHRIMP WITH SAUCE MOUSSELINE
Serves Four

4 egg yolks
Juice of 1/2 lemon
1/2 cup melted butter

1/2 cup heavy cream
32 fresh shrimp broiled in butter
Hot cooked grits

Place the egg yolks in the top of a double boiler. Slowly whisk in the lemon juice, butter and heavy cream. Cook over boiling water for 5 minutes or until thickened, whisking constantly. Place the shrimp on a bed of hot cooked grits and pour the sauce over the top.

• • • • •

THE OLD POST OFFICE'S GRITS
Serves Four

3 cups milk
3 cups water
1/4 cup butter

1 cup grits
1 cup cream
1 tablespoon salt

Combine the milk, water and butter in a heavy saucepan. Bring to a boil over medium heat. Add the grits. Bring to a boil, stirring frequently. Reduce the heat to low. Cook for 5 to 10 minutes or until thick, stirring occasionally. Add the cream and salt. Cook for 10 to 15 minutes longer or until of the desired consistency.

• • • • •

THE OLD POST OFFICE'S OYSTER SKILLET ROAST
Serves Four

2 cloves of garlic, finely chopped
4 sprigs fresh parsley, finely
  chopped
2 shallots, finely chopped

2 tablespoons melted butter
1 tablespoon fresh lemon juice
Salt to taste
24 shucked oysters

Combine the garlic, parsley, shallots, butter, lemon juice and salt in a bowl and mix well. Pour into a 6-inch ovenproof skillet or baking dish. Add the oysters. Bake at 400 degrees for 20 to 30 minutes or until the edges of the oysters are curled and the liquid content is bubbling. Serve with a toasted French baguette.

The Old Post Office, located on Edisto Island, is a short scenic drive from Charleston. It boasts one of the East's finest chefs, Philip Bardin, who cooks up their special "Fine Southern Cuisine." Well worth the drive for a dinner to remember.

CHEF LEO'S MAVERICK GRITS
Serves Four

4 cups water
$1/2$ teaspoon salt
1 tablespoon butter
1 to $1^1/2$ cups stone-ground grits

$1/4$ cup cream
1 tablespoon butter
Topping

Bring the water, salt and 1 tablespoon butter to a boil in a saucepan over medium heat. Stir in the grits. Reduce the heat to low. Cook for 40 minutes or until the grits are thick and creamy, stirring occasionally. Remove from the heat. Stir in the cream and remaining 1 tablespoon butter. Keep warm until serving time. Spoon the grits onto 4 serving plates in equal portions. Place 2 scallops and 3 shrimp on each serving. Spoon equal portions of the Topping over each serving.

TOPPING

4 ounces (4 tablespoons) julienned
  country ham
4 ounces smoked pork sausage,
  cut into circles
1 teaspoon butter
8 sea scallops
12 shrimp, peeled, deveined

$1/8$ teaspoon minced fresh garlic
Pinch of Cajun spice
$1/4$ cup diced, seeded fresh tomato
$1/1$ cup minced green onions
1 tablespoon water
1 tablespoon butter

Sauté the ham and sausage in 1 teaspoon butter in a skillet. Add the scallops and shrimp. Sauté for 1 to 2 minutes. Add the garlic and Cajun spice. Sauté for 30 seconds. Stir in the tomato, green onions, water and remaining 1 tablespoon butter. Cook until the butter is melted, stirring constantly.

SALSA TOPPING FOR FISH

1/4 cup olive oil
1 tablespoon balsamic
  vinegar
1 tablespoon chopped
  shallots
1 clove of garlic, minced
2 tablespoons minced
  parsley
20 fresh basil leaves
1/4 teaspoon each salt and
  pepper
2 fresh tomatoes, peeled,
  seeded, chopped

Combine the olive oil, vinegar, shallots, garlic, parsley, basil, salt and pepper in a bowl and whisk to mix. Stir in the tomatoes. Serve over grilled fish. Garnish with basil.

YONGE'S ISLAND SEAFOOD LASAGNA
Serves Six

1 large yellow onion, chopped
4 cloves of garlic, minced
3 tablespoons olive oil
5 cups canned plum tomatoes,
  packed in purée
1/2 cup dry white wine
1/2 cup chopped fresh basil
Salt and pepper to taste
1 cup heavy whipping cream
1 pound peeled shrimp, briefly
  poached
1 pound scallops, briefly poached
36 mussels, steamed, shelled
(optional)

1 1/4 pounds lasagna noodles
2 cups ricotta cheese
8 ounces cream cheese, softened
2 eggs
1 (16-ounce) package fresh spinach,
  cooked, drained, chopped
1 pound lump crab meat, shredded
1 red bell pepper, finely chopped
1 bunch green onions, sliced
1/2 cup chopped fresh basil
1 1/2 pounds mozzarella cheese,
  shredded

Sauté the onion and garlic in the olive oil in a large skillet over medium heat. Add the tomatoes and purée. Cook for 5 minutes, stirring occasionally. Stir in the wine, 1/2 cup basil, salt and pepper. Simmer over low heat for 45 minutes, stirring occasionally. Stir in the cream, shrimp, scallops and mussels. Simmer for 5 minutes. Remove from the heat. Cook the lasagna noodles using the package directions; drain. For the filling, combine the ricotta cheese, cream cheese and eggs in a bowl and beat well with a wooden spoon. Stir in the spinach, crab meat, red pepper, green onions, 1/2 cup basil and salt and pepper to taste. Layer some tomato sauce without any shellfish in a large buttered baking dish. Alternate layers of lasagna noodles, spinach filling, shellfish sauce and mozzarella cheese until all are used, ending with mozzarella cheese. Bake at 350 degrees for 50 minutes or until brown and bubbly. Let stand for 10 minutes before slicing and serving.

FISH ON THE GRILL

very strong. not good for milder fish

WILLIE'S WADOLTUKI SAUCE FOR GRILLED FISH
Serves Variable Amount

¹/₂ cup butter
Juice of 1 lime
2 tablespoons Worcestershire sauce
1 tablespoon finely chopped fresh thyme
2 tablespoons finely chopped fresh oregano
1 tablespoon finely chopped fresh chives
1 tablespoon finely chopped fresh parsley

1 tablespoon finely chopped fresh basil
1 teaspoon black pepper
1 teaspoon white pepper
1 tablespoon seasoning salt
2 tablespoons white wine
1 teaspoon garlic powder
Fish in season
2 tablespoons mayonnaise

Combine the butter and lime juice in a saucepan. Cook over low heat, stirring to mix. Add the Worcestershire sauce, thyme, oregano, chives, parsley, basil, black and white pepper, salt, wine and garlic powder and mix well. Remove from the heat. Brush the sauce on fresh wahoo, dolphin, tuna or kingfish fillets. Place the fish on a hot grill and cook for 5 minutes per side or just until done, basting with the sauce when the fish is turned. Remove the fish when the center is not quite done and the cooking will continue. This will prevent the fish from drying out. Heat the sauce over low heat again. Whisk in the mayonnaise. Spoon the sauce over the grilled fish and serve.

· · · · ·

GROUPER ALGIERS
Serves Six

1¹/₂ to 2 pounds grouper
¹/₈ teaspoon salt
1 tablespoon ground cumin
3 tablespoons olive oil

Juice of 2 lemons
2 cloves of garlic, minced
¹/₄ teaspoon cayenne pepper
1 large tomato, sliced

Rinse the grouper; pat dry with paper towels. Place in an oiled 9x12-inch baking dish. Sprinkle with salt. Whisk together the next 5 ingredients in a bowl. Place the tomato slices on the grouper. Pour the marinade over the grouper. Bake, covered, at 375 degrees for 20 minutes or until the fish is white and flakes easily. Serve garnished with lemon wedges and parsley.

CYPRESS GARDENS

The early settlers of the South Carolina Lowcountry referred to the mysterious cypress swamps as "weird, impenetrable places," breeding grounds for frightful alligators, and "pestilential gnats, called mosquitos." But then they realized that, when dammed, the flooded forests could serve as natural fresh water reservoirs for lucrative rice plantations. One of the early rice plantations on the Cooper River was Dean Hall, named by Sir Alexander Nesbett of Dean, a Scottish baronet who acquired it in 1725. Benjamin R. Kittredge of New York bought Dean Hall in 1909 for a winter home. Kittredge and his family developed the rice reserves as water gardens, enhancing the natural beauty of the moss-draped cypress trees and still waters by planting azaleas and other exotic flowering shrubs on small islands in the swamp. Visitors were conveyed in small boats through this paradise of eerie loveliness which became famous as Cypress Gardens. The family opened the gardens to the public in 1932, and gave them to the City of Charleston in 1963. The City recently turned over the operation of Cypress Gardens to Berkeley County.

Desserts

DESSERTS

CHEF RAMONA MEASOM'S
CORNMEAL UPSIDE-DOWN CAKE

Serves Fourteen

3 cups butter, softened
1 cup sugar
1/2 cup packed brown sugar
10 eggs
2 teaspoons vanilla extract
4 cups cake flour

2 cups yellow cornmeal
2 teaspoons salt
1 tablespoon baking powder
Fresh pineapple slices or peach
  halves

Cream the butter, sugar and brown sugar in a mixer bowl until light and fluffy. Beat in the eggs 1 at a time. Add the vanilla and mix well. Combine the flour, cornmeal, salt and baking powder in a bowl and mix well. Add to the creamed mixture, stirring just until mixed. Grease a large cake pan and place pineapple slices or peach halves on the bottom. Top with the batter. Bake at 350 degrees for 45 minutes or until the cake tests done. Cool in the pan for several minutes. Cut into servings. Invert onto a serving plate. May substitute your favorite fruit for the pineapple or peaches.

▪ ▪ ▪ ▪ ▪

Chef Ramona Measom was a Surgical Technician and upon a move to Charleston decided to pursue her real love, cooking. She is a graduate of Johnson and Wales Culinary Institute and has worked for Chef Louis Osteen, one of America's premier chefs. She is currently working with Chef Osteen in his new restaurant venture.

Fresh Apple Cake
Serves Fifteen

3 eggs
2 cups sugar
1½ cups vegetable oil
3 cups flour
1 teaspoon salt
1 teaspoon baking soda
1 teaspoon cinnamon

1 tablespoon vanilla extract
1 cup coarsely chopped nuts
3 cups chopped peeled apples
½ cup orange juice
½ cup sugar
¼ cup margarine
1 tablespoon rum

Cream the eggs and 2 cups sugar in a mixer bowl. Add the oil and beat well. Combine the flour, salt, baking soda and cinnamon in a bowl and mix well. Add to the creamed mixture and beat well. Stir in the vanilla, nuts and apples. Pour into a greased 9x13-inch cake pan. Bake at 350 degrees for 45 minutes or until the cake tests done. Combine the orange juice, ½ cup sugar and margarine in a saucepan. Bring to a boil, stirring frequently. Stir in the rum. Pierce some holes in the top of the hot cake with a wooden pick and pour the topping over the hot cake.

• • • • •

Dutch Marble Cream Cake
Serves Sixteen

6 eggs, at room temperature
3 cups plus 3 tablespoons sugar
2 teaspoons vanilla extract
3 cups cake flour
1 tablespoon baking powder

¼ teaspoon salt
1¾ cups heavy whipping cream
⅔ cup Dutch-process baking cocoa
¼ cup heavy whipping cream

Beat the eggs at high speed in a mixer bowl for 5 to 6 minutes. Add the sugar and vanilla gradually, beating until the sugar is dissolved. Combine the flour, baking powder and salt in a bowl and mix well. Add to the sugar mixture alternately with 1¾ cups cream, mixing well after each addition. Pour about ⅔ of the batter into a separate bowl. Add the cocoa and remaining ¼ cup cream to the remaining batter and beat well. Spray a 10-inch tube pan with nonstick baking spray. Layer the plain batter and chocolate batter ½ at a time in the prepared pan. Swirl with a wooden skewer to marbleize. Bake at 350 degrees on the lower oven rack for 50 to 60 minutes or until the cake tests done. Cool in the pan for 10 to 15 minutes. Invert onto a serving plate.

GERMAN CHOCOLATE CAKE
Serves Fifteen

1 (4-ounce) package sweet baking
  chocolate
$1/2$ cup water
1 teaspoon vanilla extract
1 cup butter or margarine, softened
2 cups sugar
4 egg yolks

3 cups sifted cake flour
1 teaspoon baking soda
$1/2$ teaspoon salt
1 cup buttermilk
4 egg whites, stiffly beaten
Coconut-Pecan Frosting

Bring the chocolate and water to a boil in a saucepan. Cook until the chocolate is melted, stirring constantly. Let stand until cool. Stir in the vanilla. Cream the butter and sugar in a mixer bowl until light and fluffy. Beat in the egg yolks 1 at a time. Add the chocolate mixture and mix well. Combine the cake flour, baking soda and salt in a bowl and mix well. Add to the creamed mixture alternately with the buttermilk, mixing well after each addition. Fold in the egg whites. Pour into 3 greased and floured 9-inch round cake pans lined with waxed paper. Bake at 350 degrees for 30 to 35 minutes or until the cake tests done. Cool in the pans for several minutes. Invert onto wire racks to cool completely. Spread the Coconut-Pecan Frosting between the layers and over the top and side of the cooled cake.

COCONUT - PECAN FROSTING

$1^1/3$ cups evaporated milk
$1^1/3$ cups sugar
4 egg yolks
$2/3$ cup butter or margarine

$1^1/2$ teaspoons vanilla extract
$1^1/3$ cups flaked coconut
$1^1/3$ cups toasted chopped pecans

Combine the evaporated milk, sugar, egg yolks and butter in a heavy saucepan and bring to a boil over medium heat. Cook for 12 minutes, stirring constantly. Add the vanilla, coconut and pecans. Stir until the frosting is cool and of spreading consistency.

AUNT HATTIE'S CHOCOLATE CAKE
Serves Thirty

1 cup butter or margarine
2¹/₂ tablespoons baking cocoa
1 cup water
2 eggs
2 cups sugar

¹/₂ cup sour cream
2 cups flour
1 teaspoon baking soda
1¹/₂ teaspoons vanilla extract
Aunt Hattie's Frosting

Combine the butter, cocoa and water in a saucepan and bring to a boil over medium heat, stirring constantly. Beat the eggs and sugar in a mixer bowl until fluffy. Add the sour cream and beat well. Mix the flour and baking soda together. Add with the vanilla to the sour cream mixture. Pour in the boiled mixture gradually, mixing well after each addition. The batter will be thin. Pour into a greased and floured 10x15-inch cake pan. Bake at 350 degrees for 25 minutes or until the cake tests done. Pour Aunt Hattie's Frosting over the hot cake and spread with a knife.

AUNT HATTIE'S FROSTING

¹/₂ cup butter or margarine
6 tablespoons whipping cream
2¹/₂ tablespoons baking cocoa
1 (1-pound) package confectioners'
  sugar

1¹/₂ teaspoons vanilla extract
1 cup finely chopped pecans,
  toasted

Combine the butter, whipping cream and cocoa in a saucepan and bring to a boil over medium heat, stirring constantly. Remove from the heat. Add the confectioners' sugar gradually, beating with a wire whisk until well mixed. Add the vanilla and pecans, mixing well. Pecans have a better flavor if toasted in a baking dish in a 350-degree oven for 5 to 10 minutes before using in any recipe. Cool and store in an airtight container in the refrigerator.

CREAM CHEESE FROSTING

8 ounces cream cheese,
  softened
1/2 cup margarine, softened
1 teaspoon vanilla extract
1 (1-pound) package
  confectioners' sugar,
  sifted

Combine the cream cheese, margarine, vanilla and confectioners' sugar in a mixer bowl and beat until well blended.

SOUR CREAM POUND CAKE
Serves Sixteen

1 cup butter, softened
3 cups sugar
6 eggs
1 teaspoon salt
3 cups flour

1 cup sour cream
1 tablespoon vanilla extract
1 teaspoon lemon extract
2 teaspoons almond extract

Cream the butter and sugar in a mixer bowl until light and fluffy. Beat in the eggs 1 at a time. Sift the salt and flour together. Add the flour mixture and sour cream alternately to the creamed mixture, beginning and ending with the flour mixture. Add the extracts and mix well. Pour into a greased and floured 10-inch tube pan. Bake at 300 degrees for 1 1/2 hours or until the cake tests done and is golden brown. Cool in the pan for several minutes. Invert onto a serving plate. May add 3 heaping tablespoons baking cocoa to the flour and salt before sifting for a Chocolate Pound Cake.

• • • • •

PUMPKIN CAKE
Serves Forty-Eight

1 cup vegetable oil
2 cups sugar
4 eggs, beaten
2 cups canned pumpkin
1/2 teaspoon salt
2 teaspoons baking soda

2 teaspoons cinnamon
2 cups flour
2 teaspoons vanilla extract
2 teaspoons lemon extract
Cream Cheese Frosting (at left)

Beat the oil and sugar in a mixer bowl. Add the eggs and pumpkin; beat well. Sift the salt, baking soda, cinnamon and flour together. Add to the sugar mixture and beat well. Add the vanilla and lemon extract and mix well. Pour into a greased and floured 12x16-inch cake pan. Bake at 325 degrees for 30 minutes or until the cake tests done. Place on a wire rack until cool. Spread the Cream Cheese Frosting over the cake.

THE OLD POST OFFICE'S
CHARLESTON CHEWY CAKE
Serves Fifteen

¹/₂ cup melted butter
2 cups packed light brown sugar
2 eggs
¹/₂ teaspoon salt

2 cups sifted flour
1 teaspoon vanilla extract
1 cup pecans

Combine the butter and brown sugar in a mixer bowl and beat well. Beat in the eggs 1 at a time. Add the salt and sifted flour, mixing well. Stir in the vanilla and pecans. Pour into a greased and floured 9x13-inch cake pan. Bake at 325 degrees for 30 minutes or until the cake tests done. Cut into bars.

■ ■ ■ ■ ■

*The Old Post Office, located on Edisto Island, a short
scenic drive from Charleston, boasts one of the East's finest chefs,
Philip Bardin. Chef Bardin cooks up their special "Fine Southern Cuisine."
Well worth the drive for a meal to remember.*

AMARETTO CHEESECAKE
Serves Sixteen

1½ cups graham cracker crumbs	4 eggs
2 tablespoons sugar	⅓ cup amaretto
1 teaspoon cinnamon	1 cup sour cream
¼ cup butter, softened	1 tablespoons plus 1 teaspoon sugar
24 ounces cream cheese, softened	1 tablespoon amaretto
1 cup sugar	¼ cup toasted slivered almonds

Combine the graham cracker crumbs, 2 tablespoons sugar, cinnamon and butter in a bowl and mix well. Press onto bottom and up side of a greased 9-inch springform pan. Beat the cream cheese in a mixer bowl until light and fluffy. Add 1 cup sugar gradually, beating constantly. Beat in the eggs 1 at a time. Stir in ⅓ cup amaretto. Pour into the prepared pan. Bake at 375 degrees for 45 to 50 minutes. It is better to undercook than overcook. Combine the sour cream, remaining sugar and remaining amaretto in a bowl and mix well. Drizzle over the cake. Sprinkle with the almonds. Bake at 500 degrees for 5 minutes. Cool to room temperature. Chill in the refrigerator for 24 hours. Remove the side of the pan before serving.

▪ ▪ ▪ ▪ ▪

PRALINE CHEESECAKE
Serves Sixteen

1¼ cups crushed zwieback	1⅓ cups packed brown sugar
¼ cup sugar	¾ cup half-and-half
½ cup chopped pecans	3 tablespoons flour
⅓ cup melted butter	2 teaspoons vanilla extract
32 ounces cream cheese, softened	4 eggs

Combine the zwieback crumbs, sugar, pecans and melted butter in a bowl and mix well. Press onto bottom and up side of a greased 9-inch springform pan. Bake at 350 degrees for 10 minutes. Cool. Beat the cream cheese in a mixer bowl until light and fluffy. Add the brown sugar, half-and-half, flour and vanilla, beating constantly. Beat in the eggs 1 at a time. Pour into the cooled crust. Bake at 350 degrees for 60 minutes. Reduce the oven temperature to 325 degrees. Bake for 15 minutes longer. Cool in the pan for 30 minutes. Remove the side of the springform pan. Chill in the refrigerator. May wrap and store in the freezer. Thaw in the refrigerator before serving.

BAKLAVA
Makes Sixty

1 pound walnuts, finely ground
1/2 cup sugar
1 teaspoon cinnamon
1/4 teaspoon nutmeg

1 1/2 teaspoons orange extract
1 pound phyllo dough
1 1/2 to 2 cups melted butter
Baklava Syrup

Combine the ground walnuts, sugar, cinnamon, nutmeg and orange extract in a bowl and mix well. Reserve 4 sheets of phyllo dough for the top. Layer 4 sheets of phyllo dough in a buttered 10x15-inch baking dish, brushing each sheet of dough with melted butter. Sprinkle with a portion of the walnut mixture. Continue layering with 3 sheets of phyllo dough, brushing each with melted butter and sprinkling the third sheet with walnut mixture until all of the phyllo dough and walnut mixture are used. Top with the reserved 4 sheets of phyllo dough, brushing each with melted butter. Chill, covered, in the refrigerator for 30 minutes. Cut into diamond-shaped pieces. Bake at 350 degrees for 45 minutes or until light brown. Pour the chilled Baklava Syrup over the hot pastry slowly until completely absorbed. Cool completely. Cover with foil (not plastic). Let stand for 24 hours. Cut again and remove from the baking dish. Store upside down with waxed paper between the layers. Refrigerate or freeze.

BAKLAVA SYRUP

3 cups sugar
1 1/2 cups water
Juice of 1/2 lemon

1/2 cinnamon stick
1 cup honey
1 1/2 teaspoons orange extract

Combine the sugar, water, lemon juice and cinnamon in a saucepan and bring to a boil over medium heat. Boil for 10 minutes, stirring frequently. Stir in the honey and orange extract. Simmer for 5 minutes longer, stirring frequently. Discard the cinnamon stick. Cool and chill in the refrigerator.

PUMPKIN BARS
Serves Thirty

4 eggs
1²/₃ cups sugar
1 cup vegetable oil
1 (16-ounce) can pumpkin
2 cups flour
2 teaspoons baking powder
2 teaspoons cinnamon

1 teaspoon salt
1 teaspoon baking soda
3 ounces cream cheese, softened
¹/₂ cup margarine, softened
1 teaspoon vanilla extract
2 cups confectioners' sugar

Beat the first 4 ingredients in a mixer bowl until light and fluffy. Sift the flour, baking powder, cinnamon, salt and baking soda together. Add to the pumpkin mixture; beat well. Pour into an ungreased 10x15-inch baking pan. Bake at 350 degrees for 25 minutes. Cool on a wire rack. Beat the remaining ingredients in a mixer bowl until of spreading consistency. Spread the frosting over the top. Cut into bars.

▪ ▪ ▪ ▪ ▪

FROSTY STRAWBERRY SQUARES
Serves Fifteen

1 cup sifted flour
¹/₄ cup packed brown sugar
¹/₂ cup chopped walnuts
¹/₂ cup melted butter
2 egg whites

1 cup sugar
2 cups sliced fresh strawberries
2 teaspoons lemon juice
1 cup heavy cream, whipped

Combine the flour, brown sugar, walnuts and melted butter in a bowl and mix well. Spread evenly in a shallow baking pan. Bake at 350 degrees for 20 minutes, stirring occasionally. Sprinkle ²/₃ of the crumbled walnut mixture in a buttered 9x13-inch baking dish. Beat the egg whites, sugar, strawberries and lemon juice at high speed in a mixer bowl for 10 minutes or until stiff peaks form. Fold in the whipped cream. Spread over the crumbled walnut mixture. Top with the remaining ¹/₃ mixture. Freeze for 6 hours to overnight. Cut into squares. Garnish with fresh strawberries. May substitute one 10-ounce package partially thawed frozen strawberries for the 2 cups fresh strawberries.

GRANDMOTHER'S RECIPE

The Benne Cookies are from my grandmother's recipe, being divulged for the first time! We always get oohs and aahhs! The secret is in the "whacking" which flattens the cookies to paper thinness. Speed up the baking by using 2 cookie sheets and multiple sheets of foil. The cookies can be dropped onto the foil and then it can be placed on the cookie sheet after the baked cookies are removed.

WORLD'S BEST COOKIES
Makes Seventy-Two

1 cup butter, softened
1 cup sugar
1 cup packed brown sugar
1 egg
1 cup vegetable oil
1 cup quick-cooking oats
1 cup crushed cornflakes
1/2 cup coconut
1/2 cup chopped nuts
1 teaspoon vanilla extract
3 1/2 cups flour
1 teaspoon baking soda
1 teaspoon salt
1 cup (or more) sifted confectioners' sugar

Cream the butter, sugar and brown sugar in a mixer bowl until light and fluffy. Add the egg and oil; beat well. Stir in the oats, cornflake crumbs, coconut, nuts, vanilla and a mixture of the flour, baking soda and salt. Shape into balls; dust with the confectioners' sugar and place on a cookie sheet. Bake at 325 degrees for 12 minutes or until the edge of the cookies is light brown. Cool on the cookie sheet for several minutes. Remove to a wire rack to cool completely.

▪ ▪ ▪ ▪ ▪

BENNE COOKIES
Makes Sixty-Four

1/2 cup melted butter
1 cup sugar
1/2 cup flour
1/2 teaspoon salt
1/4 teaspoon baking powder
1 teaspoon vanilla extract
1 egg
3/4 cup sesame seeds

Beat the butter and sugar in a mixer bowl. Add a mixture of flour, salt and baking powder; beat well. Add the vanilla and egg and beat well. Stir in the sesame seeds. Line a cookie sheet with foil. Do not grease. Drop the dough by teaspoonfuls 2 inches apart onto the foil. The cookies will spread. Bake at 350 degrees for 5 to 6 minutes but watch carefully. When the cookies begin to bubble, remove from the oven using a hot pad and whack the cookie sheet hard onto the counter. Bake for 1 minute longer or until the edge of the cookies start to brown. Slide the foil with the cookies onto a wire rack to cool completely. Peel the foil from the cooled cookies.

CHOCOLATE CHUBBIES
Makes Twenty-Five

8 (1-ounce) squares semisweet
  chocolate
3 (1-ounce) squares unsweetened
  chocolate
1/2 cup unsalted butter
3 large eggs, at room temperature
1 1/4 cups sugar

2 teaspoons vanilla extract
2/3 cup flour
1/2 teaspoon baking powder
1/4 teaspoon salt
1 1/2 cups semisweet chocolate chips
1 1/2 cups chopped toasted walnuts
1 1/2 cups chopped toasted pecans

Combine the semisweet chocolate, unsweetened chocolate and butter in the top of a double boiler. Heat over simmering water until melted, stirring occasionally. Remove from the heat; cool to room temperature. Beat the eggs and sugar in a mixer bowl until ribbons form when the beaters are lifted. Beat in the chocolate mixture and vanilla. Mix the flour, baking powder and salt together. Stir into the chocolate mixture just until combined. Stir in the chocolate chips, walnuts and pecans. Drop the dough by 1/4 cupfuls 2 inches apart onto 3 greased cookie sheets. Do not flatten. Bake at 325 degrees for 10 to 12 minutes or until the cookies are barely firm and the tops are dry and slightly cracked. Cool on the cookie sheets for 2 minutes. Remove to a wire rack to cool completely.

■ ■ ■ ■ ■

CHOCOLATE CHIP MERINGUES
Makes Twenty-Four

4 egg whites
1 cup sugar
1/2 teaspoon vanilla extract
1/4 teaspoon cream of tartar

1/8 teaspoon salt
6 tablespoons miniature semisweet
  chocolate chips

Beat the egg whites in a mixer bowl until soft peaks form. Add 1/2 cup of the sugar 1 tablespoonful at a time, beating well after each addition. Add the vanilla, cream of tartar and salt, beating well. Add the remaining 1/2 cup sugar 1 table-spoonful at a time, beating constantly for about 8 minutes or until the sugar dissolves and stiff peaks form. Fold in the chocolate chips using a wooden spoon. Drop the batter by large spoonfuls onto 2 baking sheets sprayed with nonstick cooking spray and dusted with flour. Bake at 250 degrees for 1 hour or until the meringues are set. Turn off the oven and partially open the oven door. Let meringues stand in the oven for 1 hour or longer until dry.

FUDGE DROPS
Makes Thirty

6 tablespoons butter
2 cups semisweet chocolate chips
1 (14-ounce) can sweetened
   condensed milk

1 cup plus 1 heaping tablespoon
   flour
$^1/_2$ cup pecan pieces

Combine the butter and chocolate chips in the top of a double boiler. Heat
over boiling water until melted, stirring occasionally. Stir in the condensed milk.
Remove from the heat. Stir in the flour and pecans. Drop by teaspoonfuls onto
an ungreased cookie sheet. Bake at 400 degrees on the middle oven rack for
3 minutes. Cool on the cookie sheet for several minutes. Remove to a wire rack
to cool completely.

■　■　■　■　■

PRALINE COOKIES
Makes One Hundred Fifty

$1^3/_4$ cups lightly salted butter or
   margarine, softened
$1^1/_2$ cups packed light brown sugar
$^1/_4$ cup sugar
1 egg yolk

1 teaspoon vanilla extract
$^1/_4$ teaspoon salt
$1^1/_4$ cups chopped pecans
2 cups flour

Cream 1 cup butter, $^3/_4$ cup brown sugar and $^1/_4$ cup sugar in a mixer bowl until
light and fluffy. Beat in the egg yolk, vanilla and salt. Stir in $^1/_2$ cup pecans and
the flour. Press into a greased 10x15-inch baking pan. Bake at 350 degrees for
15 minutes. Combine the remaining $^3/_4$ cup butter and $^3/_4$ cup brown sugar in a
saucepan. Bring to a boil over high heat. Cook for 3 minutes, stirring constantly.
Remove the cookie dough from the oven. Prick holes over the surface with a fork.
Pour the hot syrup over the dough, spreading over the surface. Bake for 3 to 5
minutes. Place on a wire rack. Sprinkle the remaining $^3/_4$ cup pecans over the top.
Cool for 15 minutes. Cut into 1-inch squares. Cool completely before removing
from the pan.

PLUFF MUD BROWNIES
Serves Twenty-Four

1 cup flour
1 teaspoon baking powder
3/4 cup baking cocoa
3 tablespoons vegetable oil
1 cup butter, softened
2 cups sugar

4 eggs
1 cup nuts
2 teaspoons vanilla extract
1 (10-ounce) package miniature
  marshmallows
Chocolate Icing

Mix the flour, baking powder and cocoa together. Cream the oil, butter and sugar in a mixer bowl until light and fluffy. Beat in the eggs 1 at a time. Add the flour mixture; beat well. Stir in the nuts and vanilla. Pour into a greased 9x13-inch baking pan. Bake at 350 degrees for 30 minutes. Remove from the oven and sprinkle with the marshmallows. Cover the baking pan with foil and let stand until cool. Spread the Chocolate Icing over the cooled brownies.

CHOCOLATE ICING

1/4 cup butter, softened
1/3 cup baking cocoa
1/4 teaspoon salt

1/2 cup milk
1 1/2 teaspoons vanilla extract
3 1/2 cups confectioners' sugar

Combine the butter, cocoa and salt in a mixer bowl and mix well. Add the milk and vanilla; beat well. Add the confectioners' sugar gradually, beating until smooth.

ULTIMATE BROWNIES
Serves Twenty

4 (1-ounce) squares unsweetened
   chocolate
1 cup butter or shortening
2 cups sugar
4 eggs

1½ cups flour
½ teaspoon salt
2 teaspoons vanilla extract
½ cup chopped walnuts or pecans
½ cup chocolate chips

Combine the unsweetened chocolate and butter in a double boiler. Heat over boiling water until melted, stirring frequently. Combine the chocolate mixture and sugar in a mixer bowl and beat well. Beat in the eggs. Add the flour, salt and vanilla, mixing well. Stir in the walnuts. Pour into a greased 8x10-inch metal baking pan. Sprinkle the chocolate chips over the top. Bake at 350 degrees for 25 minutes or until the brownies test done. Cool slightly. Cut into squares.

■ ■ ■ ■ ■

BLONDE BROWNIES
Serves Twenty-Four

3 cups flour
1½ teaspoons baking powder
³⁄₈ teaspoon baking soda
1 teaspoon salt
1 cup melted butter
1 (1-pound) package light brown
   sugar

3 eggs
1 tablespoon vanilla extract or
   flavored liqueur
2 cups vanilla chips or other
   favorite chips
½ to 1 cup chopped walnuts or
   other nuts

Mix the flour, baking powder, baking soda and salt together. Combine the melted butter and brown sugar in a mixer bowl and beat well. Beat in the eggs and vanilla. Add the flour mixture and mix well. Pour into a greased 9x13-inch baking dish. Sprinkle with vanilla chips and walnuts. Bake at 350 degrees for 20 to 25 minutes or until the brownies test done. May add raisins to the batter.

CHEF VICTORIA CORR'S RUGALACH

Makes Forty-Five

1 pound cream cheese, softened	Cinnamon-sugar
1 pound butter, softened	Ground walnuts
4 cups sifted flour	Ground currants
Apricot preserves	

Combine the cream cheese and butter in a mixer bowl and beat until well mixed. Add the flour and beat just until blended. Shape into 3 portions. Chill, covered, for 8 to 10 hours. Roll each portion of the dough into a 12-inch circle on a floured surface. Spread the top with a thin layer of apricot preserves. Sprinkle with cinnamon-sugar, ground walnuts and currants. Cut into wedges about 2 inches at the widest part. Roll from the widest part to the point and place point side down on a parchment-lined baking sheet. Bake at 350 degrees for 20 minutes or until golden brown.

■　■　■　■　■

"I used to search out the bakeries in New York City that had the best rugalach. Zabars was one of my favorites. These little pastries are wonderful for breakfast or tea. We serve them for Sunday Brunch at Atlanticville. This is my adaptation of one of my favorite recipes," says Chef Victoria Corr, who trained under the White House Pastry Chef Albert Kamin. She is now pastry chef at The Atlanticville Restaurant and Cafe located on Sullivan's Island. The proprietors, Jay Clarke and Phil Corr, have succeeded in developing a marvelous blend of Northern and Southern Cuisine.

BUTTERSCOTCH PIE
Serves Eight

6 tablespoons butter
1 cup packed brown sugar
3¹/₂ tablespoons flour
1¹/₂ cups milk
3 egg yolks

1 baked (9-inch) pie shell
3 egg whites
¹/₈ teaspoon salt
¹/₄ teaspoon cream of tartar
3 tablespoons sugar

Heat the butter and brown sugar in a cast-iron skillet over low heat until melted, stirring constantly. Mix the flour and milk in a bowl until smooth. Stir in the egg yolks and the brown sugar mixture. Pour into the skillet. Bring just to a boil over low heat, stirring constantly. Remove from the heat and cool. Pour into the baked pie shell. Beat the egg whites and salt at high speed in a mixer bowl until soft peaks form. Add the cream of tartar and sugar, beating constantly until stiff peaks form. Spread over the pie, sealing to the edge. Bake at 350 degrees for 10 minutes or until golden brown.

· · · · ·

LEMON ANGEL PIE
Serves Eight

4 egg whites
1 cup sugar
¹/₄ teaspoon cream of tartar
4 egg yolks
¹/₂ cup sugar

¹/₄ cup lemon juice
1 tablespoon grated lemon peel
¹/₄ teaspoon salt
2 cups heavy cream, whipped

Beat the egg whites in a mixer bowl until soft peaks form. Add 1 cup sugar gradually and the cream of tartar, beating constantly until stiff peaks form. Spread over bottom and up side of a buttered 9-inch pie plate. Bake at 300 degrees for 1 hour or until golden brown. Let stand until cool. Beat the egg yolks slightly in a double boiler. Add the remaining ¹/₂ cup sugar, lemon juice, lemon peel and salt, mixing well. Cook over hot water until thickened, stirring constantly. Let stand until cool. Fold ²/₃ of the whipped cream into the lemon custard. Pour into the baked meringue shell. Top with the remaining whipped cream. Chill for 8 to 10 hours.

CHOCOLATE BOTTOM CUSTARD FRUIT TART
Serves Eight

3 (1-ounce) squares semisweet
   chocolate
3 tablespoons half-and-half
1 baked (10-inch) pie shell
3 egg yolks
1/3 cup sugar
1/2 tablespoon unflavored gelatin
3/4 cup warm milk

1/2 tablespoon vanilla extract
1 1/2 tablespoons Grand Marnier
1/2 cup whipping cream, whipped
Fresh strawberries, blueberries,
   raspberries and kiwifruit
2 tablespoons kirsch
6 tablespoons apricot jelly
Toasted almond slivers

Melt the chocolate in a double boiler over boiling water. Blend in the half-and-half. Pour into the baked pie shell. Chill until set. Heat the egg yolks and sugar in a double boiler over boiling water, beating until the mixture is pale yellow and forms a ribbon when dropped from a spoon. Soften the gelatin in the warm milk. Stir into the egg yolk mixture. Cook over simmering water until thickened, whisking constantly. Remove from the heat. Add the vanilla and liqueur. Chill, covered, until the mixture mounds slightly when dropped from a spoon. Fold in the whipped cream. Chill until slightly set. Pour over the chocolate layer. Chill until set. Slice the fruit and arrange over the custard. Heat the kirsch and jelly in a double boiler over simmering water until smooth stirring frequently. Brush over the fruit. Sprinkle with almonds. Chill until serving time.

CHOCOLATE BOURBON PECAN PIE
Serves Eight

1 unbaked (9-inch) pie shell
1/2 cup semisweet chocolate chips
3 eggs
6 tablespoons melted butter or
  margarine
1/2 cup sugar
1/4 cup packed light brown sugar

3/4 cup light corn syrup
1 tablespoon flour
1 1/4 teaspoons vanilla extract
2 tablespoons bourbon
1 cup toasted pecans, chopped
Vanilla-Almond Whipped Cream

Bake the pie shell at 350 degrees for 5 minutes. Sprinkle the chocolate chips in the pie shell. Beat the eggs in a mixer bowl. Add the melted butter, sugar, brown sugar, corn syrup, flour, vanilla and bourbon, beating constantly until well mixed. Stir in the pecans. Pour into the prepared pie shell. Bake for 45 minutes. Serve with the Vanilla-Almond Whipped Cream.

VANILLA-ALMOND WHIPPED CREAM

1 cup heavy whipping cream
2 heaping tablespoons sugar

1 teaspoon vanilla extract
1/4 teaspoon almond extract

Whip the cream in a mixer bowl until soft peaks form. Add the sugar and flavorings, beating constantly until stiff peaks form.

APRIKOSEN KUCHEN

Serves Eight

1¼ cups sugar
½ cup plus 2 tablespoons butter,
   softened
1 egg
2 cups sifted flour
1 teaspoon baking powder
1½ (8-ounce) cans pitted apricot
   halves, drained

1 cup heavy cream
2 eggs, beaten
1½ tablespoons cornstarch
Juice of ½ lemon
1 teaspoon vanilla extract

Cream the sugar and butter in a mixer bowl until light and fluffy. Add the egg and a mixture of the flour and baking powder, beating constantly until well mixed. Spread the dough in a greased 9-inch springform pan. Pat the apricots dry with paper towels and place cut side down on the dough. Bake at 375 degrees for 20 to 30 minutes. Combine the cream, eggs and cornstarch in a mixer bowl and beat well. Add the lemon juice and vanilla and mix well. Pour over the baked layer. Bake for 20 to 30 minutes longer.

. . . . .

BLUEBERRY KUCHEN

Serves Six

1 cup flour
2 tablespoons sugar
½ cup butter, softened
⅛ teaspoon salt
1 tablespoon white vinegar

2 tablespoons flour
1 cup sugar
½ teaspoon cinnamon
3 cups fresh blueberries
¼ cup sifted confectioners' sugar

Combine 1 cup flour, 2 tablespoons sugar, butter, salt and vinegar in a bowl and mix well. Press into a buttered 9-inch pie plate. Combine 2 tablespoons flour, 1 cup sugar and cinnamon in a bowl and mix well. Add 2 cups of the blueberries, tossing to mix. Pour into the pie crust. Bake at 375 degrees for 40 minutes. Remove from oven. Top with remaining 1 cup blueberries immediately. Dust with confectioners' sugar.

CELIA'S PANETONE BREAD PUDDING
Serves Six

6 cups (1-inch) panetone cubes
2 eggs
1 cup sugar
1¹/₂ cups milk

1 teaspoon cinnamon
1 teaspoon nutmeg
2 cups pecan halves
Fresh whipped cream

Place the bread cubes on a baking sheet. Toast at 400 degrees for several minutes or until golden brown. Beat the eggs and sugar in a mixer bowl until light and fluffy. Add the milk, cinnamon, nutmeg, pecans and toasted bread cubes; toss to mix. Pour the mixture into a buttered glass baking dish. Bake at 350 degrees for 20 minutes or until the pudding is set. Scoop into serving dishes while still warm and garnish with whipped cream.

■ ■ ■ ■ ■

*Panetone, an Italian holiday fruit bread, is used as the base
for this bread pudding by Celia's Porta Via, a neighborhood Italian
restaurant located in the heart of downtown Charleston. This
romantic trattoria has become a local haven for the "left bank" crowd.
Artists, musicians, actors and professors all congregate here to
celebrate the gusto of Italian home cooking.*

Amaretto Bread Pudding
Serves Ten

1 loaf French bread
1 quart half-and-half
2 tablespoons butter, softened
1 1/2 cups sugar
3 eggs

2 tablespoons almond extract
3/4 cup golden raisins
1/2 cup sliced almonds, toasted
Amaretto Sauce

Break the bread into bite-size pieces and place in a large bowl. Pour in the half-and-half. Let stand, covered, in the refrigerator for 30 to 45 minutes. Cream the butter and sugar in a mixer bowl until light and fluffy. Beat in the eggs 1 at a time. Stir in the almond extract, raisins and toasted almonds. Stir into the bread mixture. Pour into a buttered 9x13-inch baking dish. Bake at 325 degrees for 50 minutes or until golden brown. Cool before serving with Amaretto Sauce.

Amaretto Sauce

1/2 cup butter
1 cup sugar
1 cup half-and-half

1/4 cup amaretto liqueur, or 1/2 to
    3/4 teaspoon almond extract

Combine the butter and sugar in a saucepan. Heat over medium heat until the butter melts, stirring constantly. Add the half-and half and liqueur. Heat to serving temperature, stirring constantly.

Pavlova
Serves Eight

4 egg whites
$^{1}/_{8}$ teaspoon salt
1 cup sugar
1 teaspoon white vinegar

1 teaspoon vanilla extract
Whipped cream
Ambrosia (below)

Sprinkle a small amount of water onto a baking sheet. Place 1 sheet of waxed paper on the baking sheet; sprinkle with water. Repeat. Beat the egg whites with the salt in a mixer bowl until soft peaks form. Add the sugar, vinegar and vanilla gradually, beating constantly until stiff. Spread in 8-inch circle on the prepared baking sheet. Place in a 325-degree oven. Bake for 1$^{1}/_{2}$ hours, reducing the oven temperature by 25 degrees every 15 minutes. Remove while warm. Invert onto a serving plate. The cake will sink in the middle. Fill the pavlova with whipped cream and top with Ambrosia.

▪ ▪ ▪ ▪ ▪

Ambrosia
Serves Twelve

3 cups sliced peaches
2 cups raspberries
3 cups sliced strawberries
2 cups blueberries

Sections of 5 oranges
1$^{1}/_{2}$ cups sugar
Cointreau to taste

Combine the fruit and sugar in a large bowl and toss to mix. Add the Cointreau and toss to mix. Chill before serving. May use fresh or frozen fruit.

COFFEE BAR

When entertaining, treat your guests to a coffee bar. Serve freshly brewed coffee and offer several of your favorite flavored liqueurs such as:

- Kahlúa (coffee)
- Crème de Cocoa (chocolate)
- Amaretto (almond)
- Grand Marnier (orange)
- Irish Cream (coconut)
- Frangelica (hazelnut)

Top with a dollop of fresh whipped cream. Offer condiments such as a dash of cinnamon or nutmeg, chocolate shavings, or a stir with a peppermint stick or cinnamon stick.

CLASSIC ALMOND CREAM
Serves Six

1 envelope unflavored gelatin
$^1\!/_4$ cup cold water
1$^1\!/_2$ cups whipping cream

$^1\!/_2$ cup sugar
2 eggs
$^1\!/_2$ teaspoon almond extract

Soften the gelatin in the water in a saucepan for 1 minute. Heat over medium heat until the gelatin dissolves, stirring constantly. Combine the cream, sugar, eggs and almond extract in a blender or food processor container. Process until well blended. Add the gelatin mixture gradually, processing constantly until blended. Pour into dessert dishes. Chill until set. Garnish with fresh fruit or whipped cream and sliced almonds.

• • • • •

STRAWBERRY DELIGHT
Serves Twelve

1$^1\!/_2$ cups finely crushed vanilla
  wafers
2 tablespoons water
$^1\!/_4$ cup melted butter
4 egg whites

$^1\!/_2$ cup sugar
1 pint fresh strawberries, finely
  chopped
3 tablespoons sugar
1 cup whipping cream, whipped

Combine the vanilla wafer crumbs, water and butter in a bowl and mix well. Press into an 8x8-inch baking dish. Beat the egg whites in a mixer bowl until soft peaks form. Add $^1\!/_2$ cup sugar gradually, beating constantly until stiff. Spread in the prepared dish. Bake at 350 degrees for 15 to 17 minutes or until light brown. Cool. Combine the strawberries and remaining 3 tablespoons sugar in a bowl. Let stand for 10 to 15 minutes. Drain the strawberries. Spread the whipped cream over the cooled baked layer. Top with the strawberries. Chill before serving.

RASPBERRY SOUFFLÉ WITH RASPBERRY SAUCE

Serves Eight

4 cups (2 pints) fresh or frozen
  raspberries, drained
1¹/2 cups sugar
¹/2 cup water
8 egg yolks, beaten
8 egg whites

1 cup heavy cream
1 tablespoon confectioners' sugar
1 teaspoon almond extract
1 cup crème fraîche or sour cream
Fresh raspberries

Process the raspberries in a blender or food processor until puréed. Strain through a sieve to remove the seeds. There will be about 2 cups purée. Combine the sugar and water in a large heavy saucepan. Heat over low heat until the sugar dissolves, stirring constantly. Increase the heat to medium. Cook, without stirring, for 15 minutes or to 238 degrees on a candy thermometer, soft-ball stage. Stir the raspberry purée into the boiling syrup gradually. Return to a boil and remove from the heat. Stir a small amount of the hot syrup into the egg yolks. Whisk the egg yolks into the hot syrup. Cool for 10 minutes. Beat the egg whites in a mixer bowl until stiff peaks form. Fold ¹/2 of the raspberry sauce into the egg whites. Pour into a buttered and floured large heavy ovenproof skillet or au gratin pan. Bake at 425 degrees for 15 minutes or until brown and puffy but still wobbly in the center. Beat the cream in a mixer bowl until frothy. Add the confectioners' sugar gradually, beating until thickened. Fold in the almond extract and crème fraîche. Spoon 3 tablespoons of the almond cream onto half of each serving plate; spoon 3 tablespoons of the remaining raspberry sauce onto the other half. Place a serving of the soufflé on top. Garnish with the fresh raspberries.

Miss Margaret's Magical Graham Bars
Serves Fifteen

1 package (or more) graham
  crackers
1 cup margarine
1¹/₂ cups sugar
2 eggs, beaten
1 cup sweetened condensed milk
1 teaspoon vanilla extract

1¹/₂ cups pecans
1¹/₂ cups crushed graham crackers
1 cup shredded coconut
6 tablespoons melted butter
1 tablespoon milk
2 cups confectioners' sugar
1 teaspoon vanilla extract

Arrange the graham crackers in a single layer on an 11x15-inch baking sheet. Combine 1 cup margarine, sugar, eggs and sweetened condensed milk in a saucepan. Bring to a boil over medium heat, stirring constantly. Boil for 1 minute, stirring constantly. Remove from the heat. Stir in 1 teaspoon vanilla, pecans, crushed graham crackers and coconut. Pour over the graham cracker layer. Top with a second layer of graham crackers. Combine the 6 tablespoons melted butter, milk, confectioners' sugar and vanilla in a mixer bowl and beat well. Spread over the layers. Chill until set. Cut into bars.

· · · · ·

Chocolate Sauce
Makes One Cup

2 ounces unsweetened chocolate
1 tablespoon butter
¹/₂ cup boiling water
1 cup sugar

2 tablespoons light corn syrup
1 teaspoon vanilla extract, or
  2 teaspoons rum

Combine the chocolate and butter in a double boiler. Heat over boiling water until melted, stirring occasionally. Stir in the boiling water, sugar and corn syrup. Bring the sauce to a boil over direct heat. Cook for 8 minutes without stirring. Stir in the flavoring.

PEACH SORBET
Serves Eight

1¼ pounds fresh peaches, peeled, pitted and chopped
3 tablespoons lemon juice
1 cup sugar

1 cup boiling water
1 cup dry white wine
1½ teaspoons grated orange peel

Process the peaches with the lemon juice in a blender or food processor until puréed. Combine the sugar and boiling water in a mixer bowl and beat until the sugar dissolves. Stir in the wine, orange peel and peaches. Pour into a 9x9-inch freezer container. Freeze, covered, for 3 to 4 hours or until firm. Break into chunks. Place in a chilled mixer bowl. Beat at medium speed until smooth. Return to the freezer container. Freeze, covered, for several hours or until firm. Let stand at room temperature for 20 minutes. Scoop into dessert dishes. May substitute one 16-ounce package frozen unsweetened peach slices for the fresh peaches.

STRAWBERRY SORBET
Serves Four

1 pint strawberries
¾ cup sugar
3 egg whites

8 whole strawberries
Mint leaves

Process the strawberries with the sugar in a food processor until puréed. Beat the egg whites in a mixer bowl until stiff peaks form. Fold in the strawberry purée. Pour into ice cube trays. Freeze, covered, until firm. Remove to a mixer bowl. Beat until fluffy. Refreeze, covered, in the bowl until serving time. Scoop into dessert dishes. Garnish with whole strawberries and mint leaves.

GRAND CHAMPION WHITE CHOCOLATE APRICOT FUDGE
Serves Fifteen

12 ounces white chocolate
2 cups sugar
³/₄ cup sour cream
¹/₂ cup butter

1 (7-ounce) jar marshmallow creme
1 cup chopped pecans
³/₄ cup chopped dried apricots

Microwave the white chocolate in a microwave-safe bowl until melted. Combine the sugar, sour cream and butter in a large heavy saucepan. Bring to a full rolling boil, stirring frequently. Reduce the heat to medium. Cook for 7 minutes or to 234 degrees on a candy thermometer, soft-ball stage. Remove from the heat. Stir in the melted white chocolate. Add the marshmallow creme, pecans and apricots, stirring until well mixed. Pour into a buttered 9-inch square pan or a 10x15-inch jelly roll pan, depending on the desired thickness of the candy. Let stand until cool. Cut into squares.

· · · · ·

PEANUT BUTTER CHOCOLATE BALLS
Serves Thirty-Six

1 (1-pound) package confectioners'
   sugar
¹/₂ cup crunchy peanut butter
¹/₂ cup (or more) margarine,
   softened

2 cups semisweet chocolate chips
¹/₄ square paraffin

Combine the confectioners' sugar, peanut butter and enough margarine to blend together in a bowl and mix well. Roll into small balls. Place on a foil-lined baking sheet. Freeze, covered, for 30 minutes. Combine the chocolate chips and paraffin in a double boiler. Heat over boiling water until melted, stirring to blend. Insert a small wooden pick in the candy balls and dip in the chocolate mixture to coat. Return to the foil-lined baking sheet. Let stand until set.

CONTRIBUTORS

Kate Adams
Nina Adams
Toi Ahrens-Estes
Martha Ameika
Mary Ann Asbill
Mary Hendrix Asbill
Caroline G. Baarcke
Patti Bagg
Elizabeth M. Baker
Charilla T. Barham
Alida Sinkler Barnwell
Lauren Emily Bates
Susan Elliott Bates
Chris Bealle
Daniel A. Beck
Kay Dowling Beck
Gloria Beiter
Guy Beiter
Tassie Bielsky
Elizabeth Bild
Clarissa Blackmore
Edith Blair
Linda Bondurant
Martha Anne Boseski
Nigel Bowers
Gay Brabham
Harriet Brenner
Sandra Bruenner
David Bunch
Cyndy Burris
Nancy Bush
Cherie Cabe
Stocky Cabe
Eleanor Carter
Susan Carter
Laura Chapman
Becky Coerper
Chris Conway
Ann Cotton
Nanci Craig
Robin Crump
Georgia Homer Darby
Susan David

George B. Del Porto
William Dodds, Jr.
Berta Donaldson
Margaret Donaldson
Nancy Dudley
Janet Eaddy
Sara Mell Edwards
Joanne Ellison
Lauren Ellison
Karen Elsey
Lou Evans
Jane Finch
Allyson Fliegner
Deborah Fliegner
Bruce Foster
Dale Frampton
Mary Gibson
Wendy K. Gibson
Harriet Gilmore
Wendy S. Marcus Goer
Jerri Gradert
Hope Grayson
Judith Green
Fran Griffin
Capers Grimball
Joe Hamilton
Peggy K. Harrison
Nancy Hart
Dixie Dunbar Hartsell
Louisa Hawkins
Jane M. Hazell
Willy Platt Hendrix
Nina Hershon
Sharon Hills
Sam Hiott
Janet Hopkins
Selina S. Hopkins
Vicky Horres
Demi Howard
Teresa Hsu
Eleanor Hurtes
Graham Infinger
Chrissy Izard

Millie W. Jernigan
Suzanne Jernigan
Angela Jones
Nancy Jones
Danya M. Jordan
Nancy Youngblood Jordan
Sue Joyner
Betsy Kalman
Harriet Keith
Julie Kelleher
Carol Kelly
Emily Kenan-Hegamyer
Donna Kendall
Mary Ann Knight
Ann Kulze
Charles Lane
Virginia Lane
Karen Lassiter
Kate Latimer
Karyn Lee
Marsee Lee
Mary T. Lee
Harriett Lent
Erica Lesesne
Dorothy W. Leslie
Jean D. Leuner
Diane Lindquist
Debbie Lockwood
Anne O. Long
Leonard L. Long, Jr.
Jan Luciano
Ann Malone
Linda Marks
Susan Marlowe
Bradford S. Marshall
Julia Marshall
Mike Marzluff
Cindy Masters
Carmi Mather
Kay Maybank
Kathy McDaniel
Doris McDonald
Kay Meier

Porter Military Academy, Charleston, S. C.

Mary Milutinovic
Virginia Mitchell
Felicia Morrison
Grace Moss
Agnes Mughelli
Lise Murray
Elaine G. Neff
Rebecca Odom
Pamela Levine Olivier
Laura Orvin
Marilyn Orvin
Nancy Osguthorpe
Beverly Oswald
Jim Owens
Yuko Palesch
Linda Pate
Sara Paul
Pam McCain Pearce
Cynthia Pearlman
Susan Pearlstine-Foster
Margaret Ann Pearson
Mary Person
Ted Phillips
Gail Pilgram

Judy Pittard
Kaycee C. Poston
Leslie Pratt-Thomas
Taylor Pratt-Thomas
Dee Pridgen
Ellen Pridgen
William Pridgen
Amy R. Pruitt
Peggy Purohit
Emily Ramsey
Marjorie Rath
Kathy Raymond
Courtney Regan
Beth Renken
Mary S. Richardson
Adrienne E. Riley
LaMond E. Riley
Mary Rivers
Kitty Robinson
Vicki Robinson
Lynn Horres Rogers
Pam Roles
Leigh Rowe
Sandra Rustin

Hamer Dillard Salmons
Joyce Sauls
Janet W. Scarborough
Marilyn M. Schmitt
Jane Settle
Trudie Shingledecker
Debbie Sistino
Callie Smith
Doll Smith
Teresa Smith
Lisa Steuer
Barbara Stone
Susan W. Storen
William D. Storen
Ann Suarez
Arthur Swygert
Daniel Tagge
Mae Tassin
June Ferrari Taylor
Peggy Dowling Taylor
Carolyn Thiedke
Elizabeth Thiem
Gloria Thiem
Andrew Thompson

Chris Thompson
Gladys Thompson
Laura Jenkins Thompson
Liz Thompson
Karen R. Titzer
Karen Ullian
Mike Ullian
Margaret Valentine
Jackie Valicenti
Fred Vesel
Julie Vesel
Ann Walsh
Mary Moore Wannamaker
Janice Waring
Torey Martin Warren
Libby Weinstein
Kay Wendell
Sally West
Margie Wheeler
Carol V. Williams
Julie Wills
Linda Wisner

MEASUREMENT EQUIVALENTS

1 tablespoon	3 teaspoons
2 tablespoons	1 ounce
4 tablespoons	1/4 cup
5 1/3 tablespoons	1/3 cup
8 tablespoons	1/2 cup
12 tablespoons	3/4 cup
16 tablespoons	1 cup
1 cup	8 ounces or 1/2 pint
4 cups	1 quart
4 quarts	1 gallon
1 (6 1/2- to 8-ounce) can	1 cup
1 (10 1/2- to 12-ounce) can	1 1/4 cups
1 (14- to 16-ounce) can	1 3/4 cups
1 (16- to 17-ounce) can	2 cups
1 (18- to 20-ounce) can	2 1/2 cups
1 (29-ounce) can	3 1/2 cups
1 (46- to 51-ounce) can	5 3/4 cups
1 (6 1/2- to 7 1/2-pound) can or Number 10	12 to 13 cups

WHEN THE RECIPE CALLS FOR	USE
Baking	
1/2 cup butter	4 ounces
2 cups butter	1 pound
4 cups all-purpose flour	1 pound
4 1/2 to 5 cups sifted cake flour	1 pound
1 square chocolate	1 ounce
1 cup semisweet chocolate chips	6 ounces
4 cups marshmallows	1 pound
2 1/4 cups packed brown sugar	1 pound
4 cups confectioners' sugar	1 pound
2 cups granulated sugar	1 pound
Cereal/Bread	
1 cup fine dry bread crumbs	4 to 5 slices
1 cup soft bread crumbs	2 slices
1 cup small bread cubes	2 slices
1 cup fine cracker crumbs	28 saltines
1 cup fine graham cracker crumbs	15 crackers
1 cup vanilla wafer crumbs	22 wafers
1 cup crushed cornflakes	3 cups uncrashed
4 cups cooked macaroni	8 ounces uncooked
3 1/2 cups cooked rice	1 cup uncooked
Dairy	
1 cup shredded cheese	4 ounces
1 cup cottage cheese	8 ounces
1 cup sour cream	8 ounces
1 cup whipped cream	1/2 cup heavy cream
2/3 cup evaporated milk	1 small can
1 2/3 cups evaporated milk	1 (13-ounce) can
Fruit	
4 cups sliced or chopped apples	4 medium
1 cup mashed bananas	3 medium
2 cups pitted cherries	4 cups unpitted
2 1/2 cups shredded coconut	8 ounces
4 cups cranberries	1 pound
1 cup pitted dates	1 (8-ounce) package
1 cup candied fruit	1 (8-ounce) package

Equivalents

When the Recipe Calls For	Use
Fruit (continued)	
3 to 4 tablespoons lemon juice plus	
1 tablespoon grated lemon rind	1 lemon
1/3 cup orange juice plus	
2 teaspoons grated orange rind	1 orange
4 cups sliced peaches	8 medium
2 cups pitted prunes	1 (12-ounce) package
3 cups raisins	1 (15-ounce) package
Meats	
4 cups chopped cooked chicken	1 (5-pound) chicken
3 cups chopped cooked meat	1 pound, cooked
2 cups cooked ground meat	1 pound, cooked
Nuts	
1 cup chopped nuts	4 ounces shelled
	1 pound unshelled
Vegetables	
2 cups cooked green beans	1/2 pound fresh or
	1 (16-ounce) can
2 1/2 cups lima beans or red beans	1 cup dried, cooked
4 cups shredded cabbage	1 pound
1 cup grated carrot	1 large
8 ounces fresh mushrooms	1 (4-ounce) can
1 cup chopped onion	1 large
4 cups sliced or chopped potatoes	4 medium
2 cups canned tomatoes	1 (16-ounce) can

METRIC EQUIVALENTS

Liquid	Dry
1 teaspoon = 5 milliliters	1 quart = 1 liter
1 tablespoon = 15 milliliters	1 ounce = 30 grams
1 fluid ounce = 30 milliliters	1 pound = 450 grams
1 cup = 250 milliliters	2.2 pounds = 1 kilogram
1 pint = 500 milliliters	

NOTE: The metric measures are approximate benchmarks for purposes of home food preparation.

WINE GUIDE

The pairing of good food with fine wine is one of the great pleasures of life. The rule that you drink white wine only with fish and fowl and red wine only with meat no longer applies—just let your own taste and personal preference be the guide. Remember to serve light wines with lighter foods and full-bodied wines with rich foods so the food and wine will complement rather than overpower each other.

The best wine to cook with is the one you will be serving at the table. The real secret is to cook with a good wine, as the alcohol evaporates during the cooking process, leaving only the actual flavor of the wine. A fine wine with rich body and aroma will insure a distinct and delicate flavor. When used in cooking, the wine should accent and enhance the natural flavor of the food while adding its own inviting fragrance and flavor.

SEMIDRY WHITE WINES

These wines have a fresh fruity taste and are best served young. Serve with: dove, quail, or shellfish in cream sauce; roast turkey, duck or goose; seafood, pasta, or salad; or fish in a herbed butter sauce.
- Johannisberg Riesling—*(Yo-hann-is-burg Rees-ling)* • Frascati—*(Fras-cah-tee)*
- Gewurztraminer—*(Ge-vert-tram-me-ner)* • Bernkasteler—*(Barn-kahst-ler)*
- Sylvaner Riesling—*(Sil-vah-nur Rees-ling)* • Fendant—*(Fahn-dawn)*
- Dienheimer—*(Deen-heim-er)* • Krauznacher—*(Kroytz-nock)*

DRY WHITE WINES

These wines have a crisp, refreshing taste and are best served young. Serve with: chicken, turkey and cold meats; roast young gamebirds and waterfowl; shellfish; fried or grilled fish; ham; or veal.
- Vouvray—*(Voo-vray)* · Chablis—*(Shab-lee)* • Chardonnay—*(Shar-doh-nay)*
- Pinot Blanc—*(Pee-no Blawn)* • Chenin Blanc—*(Shay-nan Blawn)*
- Pouilly Fuisse—*(Pwee-yee Fwee-say)* • Orvieto Secco—*(Orv-yay-toe Sek-o)*
- Piesporter Trocken—*(Peez-porter Trock-en)* • Meursault—*(Mere-so)*
- Hermitage Blanc—*(Air-me-tahz Blawn)* • Pinot Grigio—*(Pee-no Gree-jo)*
- Verdicchio—*(Ver-deek-ee-o)* • Sancerre—*(Sahn-sehr)*
- Sauvignon Blanc—*(So-vin-yawn Blawn)* • Soave—*(So-ah-veh)*

LIGHT RED WINES

These wines have a light taste and are best served young. Serve with: grilled chicken; fowl with highly seasoned stuffings; soups and stews; creole foods; veal; or lamb.
- Beaujolais—*(Bo-sho-lay)* • Bardolino—*(Bar-do-leen-o)* • Valpolicella—*(Val-po-lee-chel-la)*
- Moulin-A-Vent Beaujolais—*(Moo-lon-ah-vahn Bo-sho-lay)* • Barbera—*(Bar-bear-ah)*
- Lambrusco—*(Lom-bruce-co)* · Lirac—*(Lee-rack)* • Gamay Beaujolais—*(Ga-mai Bo-sho-lay)*
- Nuits-Saint Georges "Villages"—*(Nwee-San Zhorzh)* • Santa Maddalena—*(Santa Mad-lay-nah)*
- Merlo di Ticino—*(Mair-lo dee Tee-chee-no)*

HEARTY RED WINES

These wines have a heavier taste, improve with age, and are best opened thirty minutes before serving. Serve with: game including duck, goose, venison, and hare; pot roast; red meats including beef, lamb, and veal; hearty foods; cheese and egg dishes; pastas or highly seasoned foods.
- Barbaresco—*(Bar-bah-rez-coe)* • Barolo—*(Bah-ro-lo)* • Burgundy—*(Ber-gun-dee)*
- Zinfandel—*(Zin-fan-dell)* • Chianti Riserva—*(Key-ahn-tee Ree-sairv-ah)*
- Bordeaux—*(Bore-doe)* • Côte Rotie—*(Coat Ro-tee)* • Hermitage—*(Air-me-tahz)*
- Taurasi—*(Tah-rah-see)* • Merlot—*(Mair-lo)* • Syrah—*(Sir-rah)*
- Chateauneuf-Du-Pape—*(Shot-toe-nuff Dew Pop)* • Petite Sirah—*(Pah-teet Seer-rah)*
- Côte de Beaune—*(Coat duh Bone)* • Cabernet Sauvignon—*(Cab-air-nay So-vin-yawn)*

Appetizer Wines

Sherry, vermouth, and flavored wines are considered appetizer wines. Appetizer wines may be served with or without food at room temperature or chilled to around 50 degrees. They are usually served in a 2½- to 4-ounce glass.

Red Dinner Wines

Red dinner wines are usually served at cool room temperature, around 65 degrees, in 6- to 9-ounce glasses.

Rosé Wines

Rosés are served chilled to around 50 degrees in 6- to 9-ounce glasses with ham, chicken, picnic foods, shellfish, and cold beef.

White Dinner Wines

White dinner wines are served chilled to around 50 degrees in 6- to 9-ounce glasses. They complement light foods.

Dessert Wines

Port, Tokay, Muscatel, Catawba, Sweet Sauterne, Aurora, and Sherry are dessert wines. Dessert wines are served at cool room temperature, around 65 degrees, in 2½- to 4-ounce glasses.

Sparkling Wines

Champagne, Sparkling White Zinfandel, Sparkling Burgundy, Sparkling Rosé and Cold Duck are sparkling wines. Sparkling wines are served chilled to 45 degrees with any foods for any occasion.

Index

Tested by Time

Porter-Gaud Parents Guild
Cookbook Sales
P.O. Box 30431
Charleston, South Carolina
29417

Local: 803-723-0015
Toll Free: 800-274-8191
FAX: 803-769-7668

Order Information

	Qty.	Total
Tested by Time $19.95 per book		
South Carolina residents add 6% sales tax		
Shipping $3.50 per book		
Total enclosed		

Name: _____

Print Only

Address: _____

City: _____ State: _____ Zip: _____

Send Gift Card:

To: _____

From: _____

Note: _____

Make checks payable to Porter-Gaud Parents Guild or charge to:

Master Card: _____   VISA: _____

Card Number: _____ Expiration Date: _____

Cardholder Name: _____

Cardholder Signature: _____

The proceeds from this book will be devoted solely to enhancing the educational experience of the young ladies and gentlemen at Porter-Gaud School. They will be provided, by reason of your generosity and that of others, the tools and environment to become tomorrow's leaders.

Special thanks to James L. Mojonnier, 1997 graduate of Porter-Gaud School,
for his pen and ink drawing of the Porter-Gaud School gates, done while the artist
was a student of Jeannie Gleaton of the Fine Arts Department.

The beautiful iron gates that once graced the downtown campus
of Porter Military Academy
recall the prestigious heritage of Porter-Gaud School.